AS I WAS SAYING

AS I WAS SAYING

BY

BURGES JOHNSON

Essay Index Reprint Series

BOOKS FOR LIBRARIES PRESS

FREEPORT, NEW YORK

First Published 1923
Reprinted 1968

LIBRARY OF CONGRESS CATALOG CARD NUMBER:
68-29221

PRINTED IN THE UNITED STATES OF AMERICA

To my good friend
JOHN EDMOND MacKENTY
who proves the weakness
of my claim that specialization
kills common-sense

BY WAY OF A PREFACE

SOME men talk too much. Even in this environment I am prepared to admit it. Yet it would be a mistake not to talk at all; good conversation is a sort of mental massage. At least two people, however, are necessary to bring it about. So if I sit me down to write an essay, which Mr. Ernest Rhys says is something between speaking and writing, I must at least imagine a companion.

First of all, *he* must not talk too much—that is my business. On the other hand he must not be flabbily attentive, nodding his head acquiescently whenever I look at him. One may practice that deception in church, and I am no preacher. If he be a man, I think I prefer to have him chewing a straw as he listens. Appearance is of no great moment, but I think he has a smooth shaven face, tanned and deeply wrinkled by age and weather, with many crinkles at the corners of his blue eyes. He is tall and angular, and has spent much of his life in the open. He likes me, with a real and long-tested regard, though there are moments when I suspect a sort of amused tolerance. As for his name, it might be Silas, or even Jabez, or Ephraim.

"Let me talk," I smile at him across my desk; "it will do you no harm. I might even stir up an idea at the very bottom of your mind so that it will come effervescing to the surface, followed by a procession of others like the bubbles one sees in a woodland pond. But for Heaven's sake, disagree with me every little while!"

I would not have my book utterly disjointed, like the famous conversation that occurred in the days before the state set a limit of one-half of one per cent.

"Do you know Alferd Bashter?" said one. "No," said the other. "Whash his name?" "Who?" said the first.

We are talking about the men who talk too much—after-dinner orators, politicians, and the like; and the menace that they are to the common-sense of common folk. So we come to talk of the underlying tastes and judgments of everyday people; and then of efforts to control their freedom of choice. Then of those open parts of the country where people should have open minds; and of a certain western pride in mere bigness; and so of great universities here and there, and the making of them and the teaching in them. It was my imaginary companion, I think, who said that after all a good home anywhere was the only school of good sense and good taste. So we talked of books in the house, and other companions.

If my listener be a woman—but that needs no exercise of my imagination, for there are successive groups of them, younger ones, who listen by compulsion several times a week; and One, far wiser, who day in and day out—but, as I was saying:—

Vassar College,
January, 1923.

CONTENTS

AS I WAS SAYING

"In the woods men talk less and think more; in the city they think less and talk more. A man with an empty stomach makes all his words count for something; it's the full man who talks most and says least. That's why after-dinner speeches come after dinner."

EPHRAIM STEBBINS.

IS AFTER-DINNER SPEAKING A DISEASE?

IT HAS been said of the prophet Daniel that he went with the greater willingness to the den of lions because he knew that he would not be called upon for an after-dinner speech. This is merely an inference. But I find, upon further consideration of the prophet's record, some actual evidences that even in his early day the custom of after-dinner speaking was already well established. For when on a certain well-known occasion, he rose to address the company in Belshazzar's banquet-hall, he was introduced by the queen of the realm, who, speaking undoubtedly without notes, began very simply (see Daniel, 5: 11), "We have with us this evening one who needs no introduction."

I wish that the account might go more into the details of that occasion: as to the nervousness of the Queen, for instance, and Daniel's air of studied indifference until he rose to

3

address so distinguished a multitude. But at least it is indicated in the record that he illustrated his remarks with a number of anecdotes.

This whole matter interests me because not only have I suffered under the vagaries of after-dinner speakers, but I too have presided at a feast; I have held the wand; I know the abracadabras and the eeny-meeny-miny-mos. *"We have with us this evening a citizen than whom . . . which reminds me of a story. . . . I know you are impatient . . . but a moment of your time . . . sure you are looking forward to . . . without further humble assistance from me . . . honor of presenting—".* I too have trembled and perspired over the unforeseen emergency, or have risen panic-stricken, wondering just what the speaker's middle initial might be.

An experience on one such occasion may serve me well for a text. It was a small assemblage, with good-fellowship the keynote, and in my hands lay its post-prandial destinies.

A group waylaid me before the dinner began. "Are you going to call on John Q. Robinson?" they inquired anxiously.

"I have been so instructed," I answered,

"and his official position alone would seem to make it desirable."

"Then, for Heaven's sake and ours, find some way to choke him off! We've all heard him—and we know," they added darkly.

In those days I had all the confidence of youth. I went at once to John Q. Robinson, praying for tact on the way. But he was delightfully easy of approach.

"I wish to apportion the time," said I. "May I get an idea of how much we are to expect from you?"

"Only a moment or two," he replied cheerfully. "I have positively nothing to say to them. They have heard me before, and I am sure they want to hear from the others."

"Then shall I apportion you fifteen minutes?"

"Five will do," he said with emphasis. "Five or less."

The testimony of those protesting ambassadors lingered in my mind, and I made assurance doubly sure. "Will it offend you if I tap on a glass, or give some other indication of a time-limit?"

He was amused by my persistence. "Of course it would not annoy me," he said kindly, as to a child; "but you will find no occasion."

At the end of fifteen minutes his hearers were obviously restive, and I tapped on a glass. He would not hear it. At intervals I cleared my throat loudly. He was deaf to all but his own voice. After twenty-eight minutes I leaned so far forward that he saw me—and I saw that he saw. He deliberately turned his back toward me and addressed one side of the room. At the end of thirty-five minutes he sat down amid applause. But the nature of that applause he failed to comprehend.

All the time I was a coward, and I knew it. I should have crashed two dinner-plates together, and failing in that, I should have summoned the dinner committee and beaten him to the floor with chairs.

At intervals throughout several years my mind has recalled that experience and turned it over and over. It was not so flagrant an after-dinner crime as many that you may have known, and yet it is so bold in its outlines.

John Q. Robinson is a gentleman courteous in his ways—of that I am assured. On this occasion he knew how many were to speak, and that fifteen minutes was a liberal allotment to each speaker. His promise was solicited and given. Despite all that, he refused to heed the signals which he both heard and saw.

There is only one possible explanation: while he spoke, John Q. Robinson ceased to be his normal self; he became, in fact, hypnotized. Doubtless this explanation is simple and obvious enough to men of science, but to me it came as a Columbian discovery. I sought at once an erudite and good natured psychologist. "Tell me," I said, "how does a man hypnotize himself?"

"Oh, in various ways," was the reply: "looking fixedly at a bright object, or something of that sort."

"Listening to a sound?" I asked.

"Well, not so much that."

"Must it be one bright object?"

"Why no, it doesn't have to be bright, as a matter of fact, and it might be many objects."

"Ha!" I said to myself, "The eyes of his audience." And I mulled over the matter for a time. But the idea had not assumed a comfortable completeness in my mind. I sought my friend again, and found him still good-natured.

"This auto-hypnosis," I said, "is it actually a trance? Is it as real as the hypnotic state induced by an operator, or whatever you call him?"

"Yes, indeed, it can be very real."

"How real? How far can it go?"

"Oh, hysteria—all that sort of thing."

I think that my psychologist, while still good-natured, was becoming bored. "Here," he said, "read this. Then you'll know all about it." And he left me at the mercy of a tome which fairly bristled with the technical terminology of his craft.

Yet the Fates were kind to me. Plunging into the very middle of the book, I read persistently along, much as I go at a Russian novel, remembering how the names of the characters appear in type, but without pronouncing them. Suddenly I was jolted into an intense interest.

"The memory of a hypnotized subject has a wide range," said the book, "much wider than it has at other times. Frequent instances of this extraordinary memory have been given, so surprising as sometimes to lead to the belief that the subjects were endowed with a mysterious lucidity. Richet remarks that somnambulists describe with minute detail places which they have formerly visited or facts which they have witnessed. In one instance, a hypnotized subject sang the air of the second act of *l'Africaine*, of which she could not remember a note after she awoke. Beaunis cites the case of a subject whom he induced during sleep to tell him all that she had eaten on that day or two days before, without omitting a single item. When she awoke, he recounted the *menu* of her dinner, and she was astonished to find him so well informed. We have been able to make a hypnotized subject give the *menus* of dinners she had eaten a week before. Her normal memory did not extend beyond three or four days."

I reread the page, and then in memory I sat again with a pleasant dinner group on an occasion which may be mentioned here because it is historic, and listened while an eminent senator wrecked an otherwise joyous dinner party and his own chances for the Presidency of the United States by talking at us actually for hours, disregarding all consideration of those who were to follow him, blind to every evidence of unrest in the audience facing him, deaf to the poundings and shufflings that even their sense of courtesy could not repress. His friends explained the occurrence later by alleging a mental break-down. "Sickness," they said. Surely sickness was there, if a state of auto-hypnosis may be called an illness; and to my mind that is a sufficient explanation.

"Is it easier for a man who has once

hypnotized himself to do it again?" I asked
my kindly psychologist.

"Yes indeed, easier each time."

How satisfactorily this accounts for the
legislator who can rise in the halls of Congress
and talk for hours, recalling old addresses of
his own, statistics, quotations from the classics
—a marvelous achievement when considered
merely as an act of memory—and very often
it is obviously nothing more.

Once on a time I attended one of those
annual social occasions in New York City
where the sons of some distant commonwealth
get together for the sake of good fellowship
and the renewal of early associations. Both of
the senators who represented that state at
Washington sat at the head table; both were
to speak, and there were other speakers to be
heard as well. One of the senators talked for
fifty minutes, and the other talked for an hour
and twenty minutes, and the guests departed
at intervals throughout the evening in a state
of gloom and depression. Similarly, at a
dinner in Washington, a Speaker of the House
of Representatives held an obviously fidgety
audience of dinner guests beneath his gaze
in responding to the first toast and used up the
entire balance of the evening, so that other

speakers whose names appeared upon the program had to be omitted altogether.

Those two senators, and his honor the Speaker, and John Q. Robinson, all were undoubtedly well-intentioned, with no desire to spoil a pleasant evening for a room full of guests, or to act discourteously toward fellow speakers. But they have hypnotized themselves so often by gazing into the upturned eyes of a waiting audience that they pass under the spell with ever-increasing facility. Considerations of courtesy, sounds of warning— attention to any such disturbances as these is inhibited.

I have spoken frankly of John Q. Robinson, and I have told the true story of a certain evening affair, yet it does not disturb me to realize that these very words may come under his eye. He will never know that he is the man. When his speech was over on that occasion of regrettable memory, and he mingled with his victims as they rose preparing to disperse, it was evident from his hand-clasp, his assured smile, his every word, that he felt himself the distinguished speaker of the evening. If he had heard muttered imprecations, it would still have been impossible for him to discover the truth. He was a friend to every-

one there, and everyone was his friend. He
had come out of his trance, and the deeds of
the immediate past were as though they had
not been.

"We have to thank Heidenhain," continued
my learned volume, "for having first pointed
out the importance of inhibitory processes in
hypnosis. . . . We may then consider every
hypnosis as a state in which the normal course
of the ideas is inhibited. . . . When one idea
among several gets the upper hand, through
its intensity, or for some other reason, and
represses other ideas—"

And my oracle tells me further that the
hypnotized subject will show a definite an-
tagonism to any of those influences which tend
to oppose the actions upon which he is engaged. "The hypnotized subject," it continues, "seldom remembers on awaking the
events which occurred during his hypnotic
sleep. On the other hand, when he is asleep,
his memory embraces all the facts of his sleep,
of his waking state, and of previous hypnotic
sleeps."

The alarming truth forces itself upon my
mind that the professional orator who rises to
his feet to-morrow not only is able to deliver
all of the speech that he has prepared for the

occasion, but, if properly hypnotized, could add to it all other speeches that he has ever delivered on previous occasions. The thing is cumulative. He not only goes into this trance with constantly increasing ease whenever the eyes of many auditors are fixed upon him, but he can run longer. Truly, it is time we did something about this social custom of after-dinner speaking!

A strange custom it is, and one that has crystallized into curiously definite forms. Once upon a time a gifted after-dinner speaker told a funny story to illustrate the point he had in mind. His intentions were honorable, and the immediate result was all that he had hoped; but I wish that I knew that man's name. I would post it here in capital letters as a candidate for eternal obloquy.

"Do you know any funny stories?" says the harassed-looking individual; "I have to make an after-dinner speech." Anything will do. He will look up the stories first, and attach a speech to them. And it is another curious thing about this custom of post-prandial disturbance, that it is maintained even on occasions when no one desires it. At such times the toastmaster is drafted under protest. The speaker would prefer to be among his friends; and the diners have attended the dinner with two dominant motives: they want to eat, and they want to chat with their associates.

"Shall I call on you now?" says the toast-master, apparently calm, but with betraying fingers nervously twiddling his coffee-spoon while he turns to the Distinguished Guest at his elbow, who is trying to appear unconcerned. "Shall I call on you now, or shall I let them enjoy themselves a little longer?"

"I can't understand why those people in the far corner are so discourteously inattentive," says the Toastmaster querulously to a Member-of-the-Dinner-Committee who has come busily up to confer with him. "Couldn't you get a hint to them?"

Can't understand! Merciful heavens! They are inattentive because they do not want to listen. Of course they will conform to the proprieties if someone jolts their elbows, but they have a subconscious idea that they have come there to enjoy themselves—that this feast is a carnal occasion, where the head is to be subordinated to the stomach for a reasonable time. Their suppressed instincts have rebelled at the command that two digestive processes shall be carried on simultaneously within their mortal frames.

But after all there is as little use protesting against such established fungoid growths upon after-dinner sociability as there is in deploring the useless buttons that grow upon the out-sides of men's dinner coats; it is the fault of no one living. For surely I would not seem to blame that creature of circumstance, the Toastmaster, curiously spineless person that he is. It is his custom to weigh the happiness of a hundred diners against the possible injury to the feelings of a single speaker, and then to shirk the obvious duty incumbent upon him. Cowards, these toastmasters, and little wonder! For when by rare chance a truly courageous soul presides over the feast and it falls to his lot to dam some stream of inexhaustible elo-quence, he wins the hatred of one, whose brain-child he so ruthlessly mutilated, and the indifference of many, who never knew what they were spared. Out of any hundred toast-masters that you have known, will you not admit that at least ninety have failed to exercise courageously the authority invested in them? Not only have they not controlled the floods they were set to guard, but often they have themselves overflowed upon a surfeited, saturated meadow-land of hearers.

Nor should I blame that other reputable citizen, the After-Dinner Speaker, because of what he does while in a hypnotic trance. He and his audience are the victims not of any premeditated crime on his part, nor of any innate viciousness, but of his own good nature. True, I have heard that there are in existence professional after-dinner speakers who seek opportunity, men who actually train them-selves for such service, memorizing anecdotes and, like trained newspaper reporters, have on tap a little of the professional patter of all trades and all schools. They are an inevitable product of the system; like the hired social organizers at summer hotels they must for-mulate new recipes for spontaneity. Perhaps since the thing is to be done at all men should seriously study how to do it well. But I should like my son to choose some other profession.

A colleague of mine tells me that a young man once confessed to her an ambition in this direction. "Do you think," he asked, "I might gain in fluency by practicing, as Demosthenes did, with a pebble in my mouth?"

"Yes indeed," she answered enthusiastically; "but don't use pebbles, use Portland cement."

Probably the chief blame for maintaining the present system at its worst attaches to that securely established institution, the Dinner Committee, and with them it is often inexperience or ignorance rather than vicious natures. It might be better, indeed, if in their case the task had been studied as a profession. I remember that once upon a time the chairman of such a committee placed in the hands of one who was to preside a list of the names of those who were to be introduced. The affair, by the way, had a charitable excuse. He glanced at the list, and asked her when the speaking was to begin.

"At nine," she said firmly.

"Will any of your speakers and singers take less than fifteen minutes?"

"I should certainly hope not," she said earnestly; "they are all distinguished and most talented."

He wrote fifteen after each name, added twenty minutes in all for combined intervals and delays, drew a line under the column, and silently handed her the paper for a bit of simple arithmetic.

She looked at him aghast. "Why, that means that they won't be through until after

midnight, and many of our guests live in the
suburbs. What shall we do?"

"Leave some of them out," he suggested
simply.

"But that is impossible," she said. "They
have all volunteered their services, and they
are all so distinguished."

There was nothing more to be said; and after
all it was her party.

Toastmaster, Speaker, Dinner Committee,
all are perhaps rather to be pitied than cen-
sured; or let us say both pitied and censored.
But have I named them all? One bad habit
leads to another, and they tell me that there is
now appearing in some communities a Chairman, who in a few more or less well-chosen
words introduces the toastmaster who introduces the speakers.

These rambling comments are worthless unless they are accompanied by some constructive suggestion. An assemblage of memories,
pleasant and unpleasant, leads to the conclusion that there are two classes of after-dinner
speech. One occurs on those occasions when
people have assembled to hear certain speakers
talk at length on subjects with which they are
acquainted, and incidentally a meal is served.
If the meal is a hearty one, and the audience

dines heavily, it is unfair to the speaker. Such speeches should come first, and a light collation might be served afterward. This has many points in its favor. Audiences will be more likely to stay until the bitter end; and as even the most hardened legislator is presumably not all lung, but possesses other organs like the rest of us, it may be that the gnawing pangs of hunger will set a limit to a talk that might otherwise flow on forever.

The second class includes those speeches which are properly responses to toasts. It is these that have been so abused by custom that they come into direct conflict with common sense. Yet the present autocracy of dinner-committees, the dynasty of toastmasters, and the tyranny of after-dinner speakers will, like all tyrannies, perpetuate these abuses only so long as there is an acquiescent body of diners. We have learned in these days that the cure for all anachronistic survivals is education of the majority. Let the worms turn! If hypnotism is the key to this situation, it is in the science of hypnosis that the helpless majority must be educated, for it is, after all, their eyes that hypnotize the speaker. They have done it heretofore unconsciously. Let them become conscious and active factors in the game, and imagine the result. The after-dinner speaker finds himself facing, not an array of victims, but an array of masters. He will say whatever they will him to say, and stop exactly when they will. Let them simultaneously close their eyes and he collapses like a pricked balloon. There are pleasant possibilities in the fancy. What may we not do, Svengali-wise, in days to come, to those high-seated individuals who stare back at us from the head table?

"Talking too much isn't so harmful; it's thinking too little."
—Ephraim Stebbins.

SMALL TOWN STUFF

Our country suffers periodically from dearth —sometimes of wheat, sometimes of cotton, or coal, or labor, or money. Somehow it manages each time to worry along until the supply is renewed and optimism is fully restored. But there is one product of our soil that it is harder for us to do without than any of these things— Common Sense—and I am inclined to suspect a present shortage of it. Every great reasoner puts one and one together to make two; though some of them have now and then combined the wrong ones. In my case I have noted the falling off in the crop of common sense, and at the same time I have been informed that there is a serious social movement from the country to the city; and I find in these two things a logical sequence.

Common sense is primarily a country product. Whether you define it as sense about commonplace things, or all reasoning that is the common heritage of mankind, does not

greatly matter. Common sense surely de-
velops from a wide variety of common experiences, with plenty of opportunity for
reflection. Perhaps it takes more than one
generation of such enriched meditation to
develop it to any uncommon degree. But in
any case it is originally from the rural districts.
The herding together of great numbers of
human beings either destroys all time for
meditation, or else makes for the limiting and
specializing of each individual's experience;
and overspecialization is a great foe of common
sense. Of course one should not disparage
the expert, or lack a proper veneration for
all devotees of special research. Civilization
cannot progress without the results of their
reasoning. But for the moment my thoughts
are focused upon a more generalized sensible-
ness, for which I have an even greater respect.

This conflict between specialization and
common sense is well illustrated by the effect
of a large city upon the learned professions.
"To succeed here you must specialize," says
the veteran doctor to his young friend. "Get
to know a little more about the duodenum
than anybody else in the city, and your
fortune is made." So the young man moves
forward up a straight and narrow road of

learning, whose summit and crown is the duodenum and all that pertains immediately and directly thereto. Other roads may lead to epiglottises or vermiform appendices. Such roads and all the by-paths leading into them he must studiously avoid. The result is that he becomes a great practitioner in a great city. All sufferers as to the duodenum are sent to him, if they can afford it. Great practitioners upon the stomach or the eye-ball or the something-or-other-gland refer to him as "my distinguished colleague." It seems almost sacreligious to refer to him as a big toad in a little puddle, and yet think how small his puddle is! It is no bigger than the duodenum. A patient who comes to him with a commonplace and well located pain must either be persuaded that that pain really arises from the duodenum, or he must be sent to Dr. Jones up the street, whose highly trained and uncommon sense about such pains makes him the only other man in the city to see. In "Mr. Prohack," Arnold Bennett makes his Dr. Veiga say: "I'm admirable on the common physical ailments, and by this time I should have been universally recognized as a great man if common ailments were uncommon; because you know in my profession you never get any honour unless you make a study of diseases so rare that nobody has them. Discover a new disease, and save the life of some solitary nigger who brought it to Liverpool, and you'll be a baronet in a fortnight and a member of all the European academies in a month. But study colds, indigestion, and insomnia, and change a thousand lives a year from despair to felicity, and no authority will take the slightest notice of you. . . . "

The old-fashioned country doctor whose chief asset was his common sense may be as out of place and impossible to-day as the little red schoolhouse of legendary memory. A more complicated civilization is making greater demands than either can now supply. And yet even to-day the best type of small-town doctor is a better diagnostician than many of the great specialists who have bought their special knowledge at the cost of their common sense. The ignorances of the one may be balanced against the "accidents" of the others.

There is no particular reason for picking out the medical profession in order to pick on it. One may as readily chance upon some great metropolitan leader in the business world and find that he lives in a little puddle of dollars, with his judgments upon questions

outside his own field warped by an utter lack
of perspective. For common sense is a sort
of perspective. One who travels in a deep
rut, up a narrow road, toward a point which
is not a true summit, obviously can never gain
perspective, either on the way up or at the
top.

Your financial magnate had in him at one
time the makings of a greater man than he is.
Perhaps he could not be much greater as a
financier. The fault with him lies in the fact
that he has over-specialized, doing one kind of
thing for too long, to the exclusion of other
things. His only measuring stick is marked
in dollars. I would prescribe for him a thorough dose of rural citizenship. He had it as a
lad, and it gave him momentum. But he
has forgotten too much. In the great city he
is just a financier. In the small town he might
have been a financier, though perhaps not so
great a one, as his kind define the word great.
But at the same time he could have been a
church deacon, a volunteer fireman, a member of the school board, and even a justice of
the peace; and then he might, with all his
natural gifts, have grown to be wise.

You may cite at once, if you like, half a
dozen great leaders, specialists in this or that

field of manufacture or control, who are notable for the shrewd common sense which in fact earned them their greatness. True, and in nearly every case they got that sense in the rural districts and took it with them to the city, where it was at a premium. Then pray note how a certain change was slowly brought about. An urban public assails them with a cultivated gluttony for sheer talk; and the great inventor makes pronouncements about higher education, and the great settlement worker talks about European battle fields, and the great manufacturer settles questions about Jews and universal peace and American history, and the great politician talks about God knows what; and common sense flies out of the window.

Some years ago I was fishing on a little pond in Maine. A bit of conversation occurred on its shores that I can hear again even now— the pleasant soft twang of it, with the humorous, kindly glint in the keen eyes of the old man with whom I talked. I was untangling fish-line, sitting on the mossy bank of the little road by the pond, and puffing on my pipe as I worked. The old man, who was landlord and guide in one, came and sat beside me. For a time he pulled silently at his pipe.

Finally he said between puffs, "You're from New York." He knew that this was so, and I knew that he knew it, so no answer was necessary, and we continued to smoke for some time in silence. At last he remarked, "What's beyond New York?" I didn't know just what he meant, and was sure that the future would reveal, so I said nothing, and we both continued our meditations for some time longer. At last he took his pipe completely out of his mouth, rested it on his knee, and became garrulous.

"Folks wonder," he said, "why I don't fix up the corduroy road that runs in to this place." He had, by the way, seven miles of the worst old broken-down corduroy road in the United States. "The reason I don't is because I got all the people now I can take care of. The same folks comes here year after year. Good fishin', good cookin', good care, that'll make folks come to any place. I got all I can handle 'thout I put up some more cabins and build bigger kitchen quarters. I'm makin' all the money I need. If I fixed up that road, folks would come in automobiles, and we'd begin to get more money than we could spend. Then that boy of mine, he'd want an automobile, and my wife, she'd get kind o' restive, and they'd want me to start a hotel out to Central City. Good cookin' is what makes a hotel, and we'd get more people at Central City than we could handle there and we'd make more money, and I'd have to start a hotel down to Portland. If a man gets rich in Portland in the hotel business, he starts one down to Boston, and if he gets too much money there, then he goes to New York. An' I want to know what in hell's beyond New York?" Then he put his pipe back in his mouth.

The old gentleman is still running a fine place for all I know—the best of its kind—and he is content. But I like to think of him particularly because of the common sense that entered into all of his judgments. Among his visitors were bankers from Boston and politicians from New Jersey and college professors from any old place, in as great numbers as he cared to accommodate, and then no more. He discussed with them all of the things in which they were interested, and had shrewd judgments upon their affairs that would stand almost any test.

Undoubtedly it is well to be a great specialist in steamship shares, or the greatest operator upon the duodenum; but I suspect that

when it comes to the business of marking a
ballot, the function of citizenship is most
common-sensically exercised by that house-
holder near the little lake in the pine woods.

When I put a certain one and one together
at the beginning of this meditation, I deliberately shut my eyes to a few obtruding facts. I
gazed toward such phenomena as the govern-
ments of our great cities and the futility of
legislatures and the mad acts of mobs. Con-
trastingly I saw in my mind's eye certain
meditative woodsmen that I had met, and
wayside blacksmiths, and men on lonely
farms, and some country parsons, and the like.
And I wished that the world had more of
them and would push them up into higher
places—for men of their sort seldom push
themselves. But here are the facts I was
putting aside: that no mobs are more lacking
in common sense than small-town mobs; and
the most futilely behaving congressman or
state senator may as like as not represent a
rural constituency. After he has failed to exercise whatever common sense he owns upon
any public question, and has used his great
opportunity solely for the bedevilment of the
opposition and for the extravagant misuse of
reams of good wrapping paper by turning it

into *Congressional Record*, he can then talk himself back into office by platitudes and promises that every sensible person knows he could not possibly fulfill.

I fear that my problem is not simple addition, but something more like an equation. Men have not necessarily common sense because they live in the country. Wherever there is too much talk and men are letting others do their thinking for them, the common-sense crop begins to fall off. But the cities seem to have more than their proportionate share of talkers. Cart-tail spell-binders, after-dinner speakers, mass-meeters, agitators, pulpit orators—talk, talk, talk.

Once upon a time, so the ancient legend runs, a youth in city clothes entered a village grocery store, and with unheard-of temerity approached the exclusive circle of the elect which surrounded the stove and the sawdust box. Many incredulous eyes shaded by shaggy, sandy eyebrows peered at him from otherwise expressionless faces. "Looks as though it might rain," he volunteered, as he found a chair. There was perfect silence for a full five minutes. Finally the eldest of the senate spoke:

"Stranger here?"

"Yes," agreed the young man. "I just came."

Another long silence.

"From the city?"

"Yes—but my father was born here."

Again a silence.

"What's his name?"

"Edward Perkins—my grandfather was Silas."

Prolonged meditation; then—

"Hum,-Ed-Si- Um, Si. Wal, it *might* rain."

Too much undigested opinion comes out of the cities, unmasticated with the saliva of common sense. The country is properly suspicious of the product.

I do not claim that much meditation necessarily produces common sense. It must be meditation that follows upon a great variety of commonplace experiences—of close personal acquaintance with the outworkings of all sorts of natural laws. Our pioneers produced our greatest crop of common sense; and we are perhaps largely dependent now upon what is left over from their harvesting.

So I am coming back to my conviction that there is a direct relationship between this shifting of the population from country to city and the alarming dearth of common sense.

There is only slight compensation to be gained from the fact that the city is providing specialists for the advancement of science and the increase of personal comforts, and all that sort of thing. The extreme specialist is the only man who can get along really well without the possession of common sense, and alas, he too often does.

But the bulk of us common folk in the centers of population are being stupefied by too much talk, with no time for thought in between sentences. The United States senator who can talk for six hours at a stretch, at public expense, explaining a vote that explained itself, is emblematic of our national decline. He should be upon a high pedestal marked "E Unibus Plura" or something to that effect. Would that even now he were carven in dumb stone! Truly from this melting pot of ours arise many noxious gases.

It is so easy to become pessimistic! I believe in the innate good sense and good taste of the generality of people. But the development of transportation and the coming of the movies are taking away from the rural citizen much of his time for meditation, and now the radio will try to do his thinking for him. The city dweller who goes "back to nature" is over-prone to take a cook and a chauffeur with him, and hire several guides to meet every possible emergency due to the outworkings of natural laws.

Heaven send us a new influx of pioneers—shrewd prospectors who may find the way through great silences to some mother-lode of common sense!

> *"Any sort of sense, common or uncommon, results from minds working together. Man can't argue with Nature. She deals in facts and finalities. You can't argue a fact. You must get among folks who have theories to sharpen your wits."*
>
> —EPHRAIM STEBBINS.

YOU'RE ANOTHER

SHARP wit and common sense are two entirely different things.

"I says to him he hadn't ought to go out on strike, and he says to me what does a dub like you know about it, and I says to him, I wouldn't waste time arguing with a man whose parents was furriners."

Here is a pretty bit of debate. The question is, resolved, that to strike is wrong. The case for the negative may be briefly stated— to wit, *my opponent is an ignoramus*. The case for the affirmative is, with equal brevity, that *the negative is of foreign parentage*. The rightness or wrongness of striking has thus been thrashed out. There has been on both sides a use of the intuitive rather than the logical method; and intuition, I am told, is a sort of subconscious reasoning. Yet one might complain that on the surface the speakers did not hold strictly to the point. Little boys do a better piece of work when they cry, antiphon-

34

ally, " 'Tis!" " 'Tain't!" " 'Tis!" " 'Tain't!"

I like to converse with my fellow men. It is pleasant to find those that agree with me in any sort of opinion, and quite as pleasant to find those that disagree, if they will stick to the point. But I do not like people who think that shouting very loud will convince me, or who believe that they meet my argument by disparaging my parentage.

I wish I could assert that all persons who dispute in such fashion are uneducated. But they are not. Although this complaint starts off with a dialogue between two of the presumably uncultured majority, it is my belief that our "intellectuals" do the most of that sort of arguing. You may disagree with me; I trust you will. But I know I am right.

As a matter of fact, here in these United States our developing national habits of mind are against us. The Russian Jew, when he first comes to us, is a great debater. He can discuss an abstraction and stick to the point interminably. His forbears have been debating ever since Joseph's brethren reasoned together, and Job argued with Bildad and the rest of that lugubrious debating team, and ever since Daniel reasoned with the king. But the Russian Jews have in recent centuries done very little reasoning with kings. So, instead, they have become adept in discussing abstractions with one another.

In fact, oppressed common folk from the old monarchies are almost always better debaters than ourselves. Arguing abstract principles has been the only possible exercise of their natural interest in methods of human government. Perhaps that is why, when control of government suddenly falls into their hands, they try to put abstractions at once into practice without any compromise with expediency, and make such a mess of it. Our political forbears were all radical in their day, even the most conservative of them, but they argued principles instead of personalities, and stuck to the point, until they achieved great, constructive, working compromises.

But see what has been happening to us, long trained in self-government. Our political bulk, particularly in the cities, has necessarily done away with the town meeting, that school of shrewd debate. We have come to discuss principles in terms of candidates. "A protective tariff is wise," says Mr. Candidate. "You're a Seventh Day Adventist," retorts his opponent; and the voters are deeply shaken. "I ask your support of certain political policies," says Mr. Statesman. "You drink buttermilk!" shrieks an opposition press.

A vast number of "intellectuals" who really believed in Theodore Roosevelt's policies opposed him because they accepted a certain newspaper picture of his personality.

"What do you think of the proposed League of Nations?" I asked a lady of alleged intelligence. "He had no business taking his wife to Europe," she answered promptly.

"Shall we accept Dewey's political platform?" once inquired a section of the press. "We gave him a house and he deeded it to his wife!" shrieked an aroused populace.

Ad personam, ad turgam, ad nauseam.

But I am prepared to repeat that I have heard more of this sort of thing proportionately from learned counselors and ladies at afternoon teas than I have from trainmen, car conductors, and country grocers. I suspect, and the suspicion is based on evidence, that farmers and the followers of other deliberative callings are least guilty. This at least may be said for unionization of trades and labor, that it brings men together into "locals" where sharp debate is carried on. And even though questions may be considered there in one-sided fashion, men's minds are at the least set into healthy operation by the effort to talk toward a point.

But regardless of who may be the greatest sinner, the trick of avoiding the point in argument seems to be more and more a custom with averagely intelligent people, here and there, in city or country. In trying to suggest a reason for this tendency one might charge it up to those broad-backed scapegoats of the present moment—the newspapers and the movies. One encourages emotionalism and the other lazy-mindedness. But I am not going to charge it wholly to them, because I am neither wise enough nor foolish enough to be sure of my ground. Certain it is, however, that well-considered, well-argued editorials are finding less room in the daily press, as a whole, and less attention when they appear there, and certain it is that people whose reading is largely newspapers and movie captions meet with very few influences to counteract either emotionalism or lazy-mindedness, and both of these are the foes of clean-cut argument.

Some of this breakdown of sharp argumentation among our so-called more intelligent citizens is due to intellectual dishonesty. Broker Jones's real reason for disliking Candidate Smith is the fact that Smith once attacked the brokerage business. Jones is intelligent enough to realize the selfishness and insufficiency of this, and so—consciously or often unconsciously—his mind gropes for other arguments against Smith. The more illogical they are, the more pugnaciously he will maintain them. But his readiest recourse is personal attack. His political discussions are conducted in whispers.

All sorts of people, pleasant and unpleasant, kindly and sour, optimist and pessimist, go daily to and fro in Wall Street's historic thoroughfare. Knowing this to be true, I have always resented the outlander's fashion of assuming that Wall Street's mind is as the mind of one man. Yet I must say that I know of no place where the habit so prevails of carrying on alleged political argument in whispers— and the bulk of that whispering is like a stench that hovers over the city. Lincoln, Grant, Garfield, Cleveland, Roosevelt, Wilson are but a few of our chief magistrates who have suffered such attack. No silly bit of gossip has been too base to find an immediate listener there and a half-believer.

Greatest of all foes to good debate and clear mindedness is this tendency to make arguments *ad personam*. "That is a lie" and "You are a liar," are two statements very different in their import, and yet a great many people do not see the difference. The former is at least pertinent and has direct bearing upon the question at issue, even though it seems to lack reasoning power as well as good manners. But the latter is impertinent in every sense of the word, for it is conceivable that a liar may happen to stand upon the truthful side in many disputes.

This protest of mine is all the more earnest because it applies more particularly to that class of people which includes the greatest number of my friends and acquaintances. It would be a pleasure to have any of them dispute these assertions, but not on the ground that I am a common scold or that my nose is crooked.

THE ALLEGED DEPRAVITY OF POPULAR TASTE

"THE present vulgarity of the public taste"; "the barbarous taste of the public"—these two phrases occur in two separate articles in the current number of a critical review. In their appraisal of the public taste I wonder whether these writers made any distinction between evidences of popular curiosity and proofs of popular approval. Curiosity is aroused by weeks of skillful advertising, and spends itself in a moment. Curiosity, like suspicion, anger, or amusement, is an emotion easily aroused in the popular breast by the skilled manipulator of crowds, who usually is indifferent to the fact that it is spent in a moment, provided it is spent his way.

"Susie's Double Bed" played night after night in New York to crowded houses. Perhaps even you, gentle reader, helped surreptitiously to swell that crowd. Please analyze frankly your own motives for going. "I won-

der," said you, "why everyone keeps talking
about that play?" "I wonder," said you
again, "how bad it really is?" "Let's break
loose and be really wicked," said you to a
group of equally respectable pillars of suburban
society; "Let's have supper in some Italian
backyard and then go to that *Susie* show
everyone is talking about"; and by "everyone"
you unwittingly meant every bill-board, and
an army of pen-wielding mongers of stage gossip. So you went and ate small portions of
food from soiled dishes and enjoyed it because
it was a variation from your routine; and then
you went and saw a large portion of Susie and
came away oddly disappointed. Pause a moment in the lobby as you go out and listen to
the comments: "Not much of a show!" "Worn-
out plot, but several good laughs"; "Daring,
wasn't it? Nobody would have stood for that
ten years ago!" "Well, now we've seen that,
what next?" It is actually the fact that not
one of the many comments we overhear indi-
cates that the play has met the approval of
Popular Taste, but rather that Popular
Curiosity has been satisfied.

One would not believe for a moment that the
crowds which thronged the 23rd Regiment Ar-
mory in New York City a few years ago to view

the widely advertised exhibition of cubist and futurist paintings were a proof that experiments in these unconventional schools satisfied the popular taste. The exhibiting artists themselves would hasten to disclaim this. The public cannot approve until it has examined, and the chief conclusions to be drawn from the fact that vast numbers did examine are these: that the show had been well advertised, that it was within easy reach of vast numbers, and that the price of admission was not too high.

Let me admit here that I have no settled convictions as to popular taste. My quarrel is with those pronouncements of smug minds which we tend to accept without limiting their application, or remeasuring their value. Repeat a statement often enough and people begin to believe you, even though what you say is true. Repeat an aspersion against a person or a public, and if it be epigrammatically expressed, at once it becomes currency. "Naturally there's little good in the magazines; their editors have to please the public," says someone or other. "I never read a best-seller —you know what popular judgment is worth!" "The play has made a big hit—it must be bad!" It may be worth while to examine these common slurs upon the popular judgment, before we pass them along so glibly.

If we are to discuss popular taste in the light of theater going, it is worth while asking what portion of the public determines the quality of our drama as well as what kind it actually approves, and we must first of all focus attention on a small section of Manhattan Island. Here a little group of managers—one might almost call it a clique—limits the public's opportunity to see plays. While undoubtedly these dictators are themselves guided by the popular preference so far as they can gauge it, yet the crowds whose tastes they study are the crowds within easy reach.

New York City's theater-going public is *sui generis*. Very largely it is a visiting public. Mr. and Mrs. Public-on-a-holiday are prone to leave better judgment at home to keep house with the babies and the cook. Pew rents or collection plates are temporarily left out of the estimates. Week-enders in New York develop a weakness at the top end. The manager's problem, especially if he be a man without instinctive taste, is to arouse the superficial curiosity of this passing throng.

It is, in fact, the lively curiosity of even healthy-minded America that plays this unimaginative manager's game for him through-out. "One hundred nights in New York" is a catchword that will fetch the gate receipts in Grand Rapids, where very possibly the New York manager has some interlocking claim upon the leading theater, and Mr. and Mrs. Grand-Rapidian say, "Let's go and see why New York went!" It is even whispered that in cases where the manager of limited vision has failed to arouse floating New York's curiosity up to a hundred-night pitch he has played to "papered" houses at a loss, for enough additional days to justify that magic phrase when on the road. This may at least be credited to his business acumen. Yet whatever the manager's caliber, one would assume that current plays on Broadway ought to represent his best effort to locate the fixed tastes of his audiences. This might be assumed if each play was a hazard, a gamble on public preferences. If the manager correctly appraises popular taste he wins; if incorrectly, he loses. But it is said on good authority that in not a single Broadway production nowadays is the manager taking any risk. His enterprise is underwritten before it starts. Payments for moving picture rights, stock rights and the like, contingent only upon a few days of actual

Broadway presentation, are sufficient to protect him against any loss whatever. He is betting on a sure thing. He does not need to educate himself in public taste. He can thrive without such knowledge.

To growl indiscriminately at the theater is not my purpose, nor would such growling fairly represent my attitude. But in considering common disparagements of the popular taste in drama, it is well to point out that other factors beside general public preference help to determine the character of the most loudly heralded plays. It is possible that the widespread "little theater" movement, the drama leagues and amateur players everywhere, are not merely the passing fads of a few "intellectuals." They may be proof of popular unrest over a financial control of the stage that is insufficiently responsive to the common desires. If all butter manufactured on a large scale came under the control of a few men and they marketed a rancid product, we might accuse the public who ate it of being weakly acquiescent, but not of preferring rancid butter. And it is a safe guess that little independent sweet-butter factories would spring up here and there over the land and struggle along, despite the difficulties of distribution. It is indeed an acquiescent public, but its conscious preferences will finally evidence themselves.

The disparager of popular taste is sure to cite most triumphantly the "movies" of today in defense of his views. But all that has been said in defense of popular taste in connection with the spoken drama may be reiterated and emphasized in the moving picture field. I can do no better than to quote from the printed word of an expert—one who writes movies as well as of them. He says:

"The infancy of motion pictures has been left to the supervision of (take it by and large) the most dangerous element of our population, the element that represents, primarily, greed. Greed is part ignorance. The two are inextricably interwoven. . . . To them we have entrusted the early years of the motion picture. For this, our children, and our children's children, must pay. With the appearance of the first motion pictures there was a rush to the new field closely comparable to the rush to some new gold district when a strike has been made in most unpromising regions. The first to arrive on new ground are the daring adventurers who take big risks for the possibility of easy profit—the something-for-nothing men. The first writers for the motion picture industry, taking it as a whole, were those who happened to be on the ground or in touch with the first studio makers, *with nothing better to do*. The office hangers-on, unable to make good in their own field, willing to take a chance at anything—these were the first men to drift into writing for pictures. And, as with the writers, so with the other branches of the industry. So that, by the time the moving picture industry assumed substantial proportions, and began to attract a greater number of high caliber workers, the stamp of inefficiency, ignorance, and an astounding lack of intelligent idealism, already marked the new 'art.' The more competent of the incompetents—keeping always to generalities and avoiding the specific exceptions that mitigate conditions here and there—found themselves in controlling positions, and formed a barrier which the tides of betterment have been able to beat down but slowly. And the pictures turned out represented, in the aggregate, the low mental and moral and spiritual tone of those first drawn to the industry."

In other words, this writer suggests, as I
have suggested in the case of the theater, that
its worst manifestations, in fact its general
manifestations, do not so much reflect the
tastes of the public as the instincts of the
group which control it as an industry; that it
has not become fully responsive to the wishes
of the public, but only to the misguided efforts
of unimaginative Greed to interpret those
wishes.

The other day I sat in a crowded moving
picture house in a small Colorado city. A
"comedy" was on the screen. It was a succession of slap-stick situations, almost any one
of them so grotesquely absurd as to justify
laughter, but following one another in such
perplexingly rapid succession as to benumb
the risibilities of the audience; and it was a
patent fact that either an apathetic or a dazed
audience rather than a delighted one watched
the farce. Suddenly into the midst of the plot
was introduced an episode of unnecessary and
even inconsistent vulgarity. I watched the
reaction with interest, and I believe without
prejudice. This was a ten-cent matinee audience, crowded with children. It was a "low-
caste" audience, if a supercilious critic might
be allowed to classify it, and beyond question

it was either offended or embarrassed—probably it could not have analyzed its own emotions and told you which. One can easily imagine the process of evolving that scenario. The producer examined it, interpreted the popular demand by means of his own wizened apperceptions, and said, "Give 'em more rough-house". "Put that there young lady into full tights." "Get more suggestion into the third reel. That's what the public wants." Heaven is most unkind to its common people, in that it provides them with such interpreters.

Yet this producer is by no means stupid. If he injects enough of the startling, the shocking, the arousing, his film will advertise itself to curiosity seekers; even the police powers of the city or some crusading clergyman may give it a boost. True, it will die in a day, but in the meantime it paid and he has "turned over his capital." As long as unadulterated greed exists unchecked, such men will give the public curiosity, not the public taste, what it wants.

The present-day trend in moving pictures is comforting to those who have faith in the popular judgment, for surely the producers have not determined to run contrary to a general demand and force upon the people something

better than they want; yet everywhere producers, even the stupidest, are revising their
editorial staffs, hunting hurriedly for better
sources, and vying with each other to destroy
that ugly god which they created in their own
image and called Public Opinion; groping for a
true god which they have no native means of
recognizing.

But let us get along to books. In the field
of the theater a brilliant Belasco or an imagin-
ative Hopkins might dispute my assertions and
I should be at a loss for retorts. The publishing business is obviously in the hands of more
men, more widely distributed. A hundred
highly competitive publishing houses are striving to ascertain the popular taste and to cater
to it. Moreover, the public may send for the
books it wants (from among those it has heard
about), while it must take whatever theaters
it can get to. What sort of book does it mostly
want, and who are the buyers of these books?

My friend Jones is a professional critic. He
too, has gauged the American public. He is
fond of saying that it prefers to read "sentimental drivel," or "nasty society stuff." I
think he has specifically in mind the highly
moral fiction of the Rev. Henry B. Williams
and the society romances that wriggle through

the pages of a certain neurotic magazine. I
agree with Jones in his estimate of these writ-
ings, but I want to be sure that he is right in
saying they determine the popular taste.

Sixty million people in this country never
see a book, and only about four per cent. of our
population ever get into a bookstore. The
book buyers select from among the books they
have heard about. Yet they hear of very few,
because, for a popular commodity, books are
remarkably underadvertised. This must be so.
Mr. Gillette makes one safety razor and his
entire advertising appropriation pushes its
sales. Mr. Henry Holt publishes one hundred
books and whatever advertising appropriation
he can afford must be divided among them.
Each may get a hundredth part of his budget.
Mr. Gillette will make the same razor next
year. Mr. Holt will make a hundred new
books, with brand-new names demanding entirely different advertising.

Moreover, book distributing methods are
painfully inadequate. It is said that there are
fewer retail bookstores in the United States to-
day than there were fifty years ago. In a half
million homes where reading is desired what do
you find? The Bible, a "home doctor," a history of the world, sold on subscription by some

itinerant vendor, and then what? "Ben Hur," perhaps, and a worn volume of Scott or Dickens, and some school books. Please realize that when a new volume of Mr. So-and-So's salacious stuff is tossed from the presses next spring, it is seized upon by the merest fringe of our vast literate population. At the end of six months its sales are dead as a door-nail; yet "David Copperfield" is still selling in twenty or thirty different editions, and "Tale of Two Cities" in forty or more. "Ah," says critic Jones, "that isn't public taste, that's habit. Sets of Dickens aren't books, they are furniture, library wall-paper, certificates of culture." Jones would be right if the chief sale of Dickens were by sets, but it is not. One of the many low priced editions, the year before the war, sold, of "David Copperfield" 4,700 copies, of "Nicholas Nickleby" 2,100, "Pickwick Papers" 2,000, "Tale of Two Cities" 2,000, "Our Mutual Friend" 1,100, and other individual volumes of his works in almost negligible quantity. All this was despite the fact that every public library had them. In the year of Dickens' death twenty-one different editions of his works were on sale in America; forty-five years later there were as many as fifty of certain volumes. In that same year before the war a certain "best seller" went up to two hundred thousand copies in six months and then went down—and out.

It is easy to be misled by flash-in-the-pan successes, when judging popular taste. Mr. So-and-So's society scandals make a very loud noise and then die. Any publisher in the land, if offered a choice between the works of best seller So-and-So and the works of Joseph Conrad, for instance, would choose the latter; because Conrad's works are a better property in their second year than in their first. Let us substitute the phrase "quick seller" for "best seller" and keep our meanings clear. Two of America's best sellers in the field of copyright fiction are "Ben Hur," with close on two million sales and "David Harum," with more than a million. The publishers of "Tom Sawyer" and "Huckleberry Finn" a short time ago manufactured fifty thousand copies each of these two books, to carry them through the coming year; and these stories were first published over forty years ago. It is a safe bet that five out of this year's "six best sellers" will, two years from now, be as the grass that withered; while in that same year "Captain January" and "A Bird's Christmas Carol" and "The Man Without a Country" will approach or enter their second million; and even next year "Lorna Doone" will outsell all six of them.

What the public asks for in the way of literature is a slightly different question from "What does the public like?" I have said that it quite naturally wants to see what it has heard about. And what it hears about is less a question of quality than of merchandising. Then there is always this dominant third question, "What is it able to get?" I am not sure what it likes—but I am optimistic in my guessing.

No, the vast literate public, as far as it is buying books at all, is not buying quick sellers, anomalous as that statement may sound. An English publisher announces a new series of cloth-bound books at a low price and of a handy size, and within a few months over a million copies are sold. The editor of the series does not choose his titles from among those books whose sale in their day was due wholly to an aroused public curiosity. He finds the books whose continued sale, however slow, proved that they had *met the approval of popular taste*, and these are republished, and now sell all over again in a fashion to put the six-months-old quick seller to shame.

I have urged that one may not estimate by means of quick sellers the standards of popular literary taste. Yet when even one hundred thousand people, out of our total of readers, see fit to buy a new book within six months of its publication, that is a phenomenon that I must not dismiss over-lightly. They tell me that those sentimental novels by the Rev. Henry B. Williams, for instance, which to Jones's annoyance have sold so phenomenally, were advertised and distributed with unprecedented lavishness and skill. They were brought to the notice of people who wanted to read but had never had a new book thrust upon their attention before, as safety razors had been thrust upon their attention—or made so easy to buy. But perhaps that does not tell the whole story. Jones says, "Those books are without merit; the public buys them; therefore the public has no literary judgment." I admit that I don't like the stories but, since so many human beings do, there may be certain merits in them that I fail to appreciate. Jones and I proceed from different premises. But it seems to me important to note that certain other books by the same author, although equally sentimental and distasteful to Jones, had the same selling force

back of them and yet failed to win public
approval. Some simple quality, overlooked
by the critic, causes this difference. Perhaps
its very simplicity is the reason he over-
looks it.

When "David Harum" appeared and gradually secured a sale that was a record-breaker
in its day, my friend Jones and others said it
only went to prove the poor quality of popular
taste. Now we realize that there was in the
book an artistic and spiritually truthful picture of a certain homely American type. That
character sold the book and kept on selling it.
I have known Jones himself to sit patiently
through a great deal of bad vaudeville and feel
well repaid when Madame Bernhardt came on.
I have heard him extol Drinkwater's "Lincoln"
and quite ignore the impossible negro dialect,
or the maidservant with English manners out
in Illinois in 1859. Perhaps the public, too,
does not place the seal of its approval on a
whole book when it buys and buys, but only
upon some one quality or some one character
in the story, that it is able to recognize as true
in spirit. And it accepts, or ignores as non-
essential, certain accompanying characteristics
that to Jones may mean the book's damna-
tion.

If so, I am sure it is not any subtle element, for the popular mind is not subtle. Whatever actually suits the public taste must be as simple and as obvious as Millet's "Angelus." Moreover, it may not be cynical or iconoclastic. Virtue must be extolled, sin deplored. The popular taste prefers optimism to pessimism just as the "general public" still believes in God and the ten commandments. It is true that an indecent book if well advertised can secure a large sale. But publishers will tell you that the limit of sale, though large, is definite and can soon be reached; and no amount of skillful merchandising could thereafter be made to pay. A certain magazine has attained success by appealing to prurient curiosity. It has gradually built up and maintained a definite and profitable circulation. But that circulation is a small fraction of potential magazine readers. On the other hand, those household magazines which have run into circulations of a million and a half or two million, weekly or monthly, find it worldly wise to be virtuous to the point of vapidity; and they could, if it were not unprofitable to do so, extend their circulations indefinitely.

If I were to create a story that approached

literary perfection, and then wrote it in French, no one could assert that popular lack of interest in it proved the public's lack of good taste. The public in this instance would be limited to those with a reading knowledge of French. If my story presupposes a knowledge of applied psychology and makes use of many technical terms in that field of research, then I have again shut out a large portion of the public. My "price of admission" is too high.

A publisher friend of mine calls these superficial qualities of literature "entrance requirements." As you add to their number or to their esotericism, you reduce the number of those who can get into your book. But that limited number has not necessarily a finer sense of what is the good and the true and the beautiful in literature. Many of them may have. But some may be as blind as bats in the sunlight. You have merely a cross section of the public, cut to the lines of your entrance requirements.

I doubt whether it is any disparagement of the public's good taste to say that it prefers the simple and the obvious. Add a frock coat and silk hat to the rudimentary costume of "The Discus Thrower" and though the fine lines are still underneath you have made the statue less perfect by reason of these embellishments—and it will become still more grotesque with the passing of the silk hat. It is because of those qualities in the sculptor's achievement which are unhidden by passing fads and ephemeral embellishments that it still lives. My friend Jones would protest against such a discus thrower, but his fault-finding would be because the frock coat was not a cutaway.

In fact, I begin to suspect that Jones enjoys fault-finding. Yet he himself does not face criticism cheerfully. He does not like me to tell him, for instance, that he gains more enjoyment from the contemplation of technique than of accomplishment. Nor does he like me to say that criticism is non-creative and a parasite among the arts, thriving upon literature as mistletoe thrives upon the oak. Far be it from me to wish the mistletoe abolished—it has certain pleasing social functions. But I notice that it only pretends to have roots of its own; and it often injures a delicate oak, while it never builds up a strong one. As for contemplating the beauty of the forest, it may see only the limbs from which it draws its sustenance. Critics can too easily lose touch with the public. They are not sure what it likes, but they know its tastes must be lower than their own.

"But, Mr. Omniscience," say you, "what does the public like?"

First, something it can understand; second, something it *recognizes* as spiritually true; third, something that is not destructive of its fundamental faith in the eventual out-working of all things for good; finally, and more specifically, the things it really likes are the things it *keeps on* buying. For this last is not a vague generality. It means that if revivals of "Pinafore" or "Robin Hood" or "Wang" arouse greater enthusiasm forty or thirty or twenty years after their creation than a current light opera six months old, then they are the better criteria of popular taste. It means that any novel which sells successfully ten years after publication is better evidence on which to judge standards of public approval than one which dies in six months.

When Hardy's novels appeared, the public disregarded the judgments of the critics and, having selected certain ones for favor, *kept on buying them*. Critics now say that these certain ones are most worthy of survival. Critics tell us that Dickens must rest his reputation upon a certain three or four books. The public settled upon those books in the beginning, and keeps on buying them.

Let me frankly admit, in conclusion, that whatever arguments I may have presented in the foregoing are largely negative. I would urge that those evidences of the popular taste which you find most depressing are not good evidence. On the stage and in moving pictures, the evidence seems to me to indicate that the public likes something much better than it generally gets. In books the greatest percentage of the literate public gets nothing at all. Quick sellers indicate first of all good merchandising methods and some curiosity-arousing quality. Whatever else they indicate remains to be proved.

"What do you think of the popular taste in books?" I asked a bookseller of unusually wide experience. "A most interesting question just now for this reason," he replied. "Even before the great war the old classics had begun to give way. Few read George Eliot now. Fewer each year are reading Scott. Before long we shall be unable to measure public taste by old standards. What are the new? Live behind a book counter year in and year out as I have done and you may find cause for depression in the stuff that crosses that counter. But it is noting the character of the books that buyers still call for, two and three years after their glory has departed from the advertising spaces, that makes an optimist of me."

A negative argument will not settle anything, it is true. But as I said in the beginning, I have not sought to settle anything. On the contrary, I want to unsettle something, namely your mind, in case it is contentedly wearing certain hand-me-down ideas about the "barbarous taste of the public" without first considering whether or not they fit. If they do, by all means wear them.

"Constable," said the Lady-who-lived-by-the-sea, "those bathers are improperly clad. You must arrest them!" "But, Madam," said the officer in surprise, "they are so far away I can hardly see them!"

"Ah, but just try my opera glasses."

—CHALDEAN FABLE.

THE CENSORIOUS MIND

W HEN the millenium arrives, it is to be supposed that each individual citizen will be responsible for the condition of his own wings and the tuning of his own harp. But perhaps there will be some community clouds which several individuals will have to care for jointly, and some orchestral organizations where harmonious harping is an essential. Such groups will have to arrange for the happiest method of working together, probably taking turn and turn about in making up their cloud in the morning and airing it properly, and appointing some individual who will be empowered to pitch people's harps for them. Such voluntary agreements might give groups a limited right to control the preferences of individuals. This might call for a mild form of policing. But it is impossible to conceive of a censorious person in that ideal state.

A censor is one who must interest himself in motives. He must examine intentions, in order to prevent acts as yet uncommitted. It would not be possible for one citizen, after the millenium, to set himself up as a dictator of the states of mind of others than himself. A censor is either a man whose superhuman discernment enables him to foresee the inevitable result of the intended act of another and then forbid the act before it is committed; or else he is just an ordinary man appointed by the state to guess at such results, and act on his guessing.

The millenium has not arrived, and community living has made it evident that some people behave so badly that they interfere with the happiness of their fellows. Heaven has appointed me to be the supervisor of my own motives, and not of any other's; but I may have something to say about another's acts, if he settles near me and proceeds to live in such an overbearing fashion that he makes it impossible for me to carry out my reasonable desires. Some form of community government must restrain him, as a matter of expediency, so that decent individuals throughout the community can live their own lives. This man-made right of interference is the right of a group to control one individual, and rests upon expediency alone.

The community must act by means of some appointed policeman. This constable—this moral abnormality—is an unfortunate fellow, because he must watch others as well as himself and make a profession of it. He soon comes to watch the behavior of others, and guess whether or not they are planning to harm the community. It may lead him to assume that what they are about to do will be harmful to the community, when really it will not.

It is true that a policeman often locks up persons on suspicion, or sends *dangerous-looking* characters out of town. This is sheer power that he exercises with the approval of the majority, in times of serious unrest. No one claims that he has any real right to do it—not even he himself. He does it usually with the conviction that, if he took the time to look up the records of those persons, he would find that they had already done some harmful acts. He cannot admittedly do it on the ground that they may soon be harmful. This policeman spends so much of his time dealing with sin and sinners that it is easy for him to distrust men's motives. He may become censorious. A censorious policeman is a trouble-breeding rather than a trouble-quelling indi-

vidual. Now and then the community discovers that it must protect itself against him.
It says to him: "You must not guess at men's
motives, but consider only their acts, and if
you are going to decide all by yourself which
acts are harmful to us we will soon be more
afraid of you than we are of our disturbers, so
we will give you a list of the deeds that we are
sure would interfere with our pursuit of happiness, and you will please concern yourself only
with them. We will give you a revised list
now and then, to include the latest inventions
of unsocial persons."

There will be small place for the policeman
when the millenium arrives. In the meantime his necessary existence has this bad
effect upon society—numbers of amateur
policemen spring into being. They do not
study policing as a profession, because it is
only an avocation with them. They do not
learn the limitations imposed. They guess
at intents and they assume harms. They
cease to watch themselves and take to watch-
ing others by preference. They develop censorious minds.

It is bad enough when a policeman takes
to the business of supervising acts before
they are committed; in other words, super-

vising motives. But when ordinary members of society get to speculating censoriously upon what fellow members of the community are likely to do, organized society is hard to live in.

A censor, in the exact meaning of the word, is a man who is empowered to examine books or plays or pictures before they are published, and say whether or not they shall be published. In any other realm of human action, such a degree of police power is not granted to any individual. A published book which has actually worked harm, either by inciting to violence or because it offends the sense of decency of an entire community, is a deed. It is an act that may be proven. The community may inflict punishment upon the perpetrator, in order to discourage recurrence and as a warning to other unsocial individuals. But a book which has not yet been published has not become such an act. It is still an intent. The effect that it will have cannot be foretold.

The greatest danger that lies in the recognition of rights of censorship is that thoughtless people will grow to believe that any such real right exists. If we can make all citizens understand that a censor is an impossible person in an ideal existence, then less harm will be done when we appoint them as temporary expedients.

A censor is so easily reducible to absurdity. Instead of checking a book or a play just before its perpetration, would it not be quite as reasonable and far better to have censors who would explore into the minds of those about to write books, and slay the uncommitted evil before it is even planned? There is your perfect censor, in a social world that still breeds sinners. Every harmful play that is suppressed has worked some harm before its suppression, and the mind which conceived it is still free to commit innumerable other offenses of a similar sort. We ought to have discerning censors, who can see what is about to happen because of their superknowledge of mental processes, their superanalytical discernment. "A certain type of mind in a certain environment," they should be able to say, "operated upon by certain suddenly injected forces, will produce an improper play. Let us stop the operation of those forces and of that mind before the deed is committed. An improper play is one that we know in advance will injure the minds that come into contact with it." Censors possessing such peculiar abilities are hard to find. It is especially hard for a Governor to find them, and then appoint them to office, by and with the consent of the Senate.

Given such feeble abilities as we possess for community self-government, what shall we do to protect ourselves against the probable emanations of diseased minds? There seem to be only two possible methods that promise efficiency. One is, to forbid everyone in the community to read or see or hear things that might be harmful to him. That is a pretty heavy task in the way of forbidding. Then there is another way out. Train a community not to want to read, or look at, or listen to such things, and, behold, we come back to education. Shall we teach people to govern their own minds, or shall we proceed on the principle that every person ought to study how best to govern the mind of his neighbor? There are some lines from Scripture that have, I am sure, been frequently misinterpreted. "Am I my brother's keeper?" has been read to numberless groups of children, always with only one answer understood. It is assumed that the Heavens thundered back at Cain: "Yes, you

are your brother's keeper. Where is he?"
It seems to me that there is another answer,
and it is this: "No, you are not your brother's keeper, and yet you made yourself so
by taking his life, which belonged to him and
not to you. You are horribly conscious of
the fact that you invaded his realm of private control to the very limit to which you
could go, and now you pretend you did
not."

The purpose of education is to teach individuals to govern their own lives. That
would be a very curious education which
taught each individual to govern the life of
somebody else. In any schoolroom there
are always those little children who find their
greatest satisfaction in observing and report-
ing the sins of their fellows. This tendency,
unchecked, leads to a moral disease far more
insidious and harmful to the community
than the outgrowths of the peccadillos which
these small, self-appointed policemen reported.

There are times when I yearn for a censorship. I go to the moving picture house,
hoping to be entertained and instructed, and
my evening is spoiled by the sight of silliness
and filth from which I cannot escape. Then

I say to myself, "Oh, for a censor!" Whole communities nowadays are ejaculating the same thing, not realizing that the outcry is an evidence of laziness and moral inertia. They want new laws to do for them that which they will not do for themselves. There are two things I failed to realize when I uttered that ejaculation. One is that I was affronted by all that silliness and filth because of my own act. Mine was not a passive procedure, but an active one. I paid the price of admission to the movie theater, knowing well the type of man generally engaged in making moving pictures to-day, and the type of picture that he is making. And the other weakness behind my appeal for a censor is this: Who knows whether or not an official censor would consider those pictures either silly or filthy? We get into a curious sort of *impasse* when we build our social regulations upon the theory that one individual ought to determine what is going to be good or bad for somebody else.

"That book, or that play, or that picture impairs public morals," cries an outraged public.

Then where are the police? There are laws to suppress it.

"Our police do not act. They are inefficient, or overworked."

Then get more, or better police.

"We cannot do that. It is too much trouble. And, besides, we have given ourselves over into the hands of political leaders who benefit by an inefficient police. No; we want more laws."

What laws?

"Since our police fail to punish an act that impairs the morals of the community, we want laws providing for an official to precede the policeman, who will decide whether or not an act about to be committed is going to be harmful. If we can only have such censors we shall not need the police, and we shall not be bothered by the necessity of deciding for ourselves what we should read and what we should see."

The trouble is that there are some things that no one man can decide for another. Once upon a time—and it was long after I had reached years of alleged intelligence— I read a novel that seemed to me utterly charming. I placed it among my treasured books. Then, one time I lent it. It was evidently bandied about in the miscellaneous realms of a city boarding house, and it

came back to me with pencil marks on some
of its margins. Those marks made a new
book of it. I found paragraphs therein that
became, when separated from their context,
indecent to an offensive degree, and I mar-
veled at my own strange innocence of mind
that should have overlooked them before.
I should not want one of those borrowers
to censor my reading.

A censor must lay down regulations to
govern uncommitted acts. What recipes can
he follow? He begins with these community
police regulations: That no man may wil-
fully impair the morals of a community, or
incite it to violence, or so act that he makes
the peaceful pursuit of happiness impossible
for his neighbors. And the censor says to
himself, "I must decide what books or plays
or pictures are sure to do these things."
But the most unlikely things have incited to
violence in the past. As for perverting
men's morals, the censor has to define morals.
The majority of our community once held it
actually immoral to oppose the king's minis-
ters, and many of the clergy once declared
it immoral to attack the institution of slavery.
Many good people to-day consider it a question of morals whether or not a woman

should smoke. Many do not so consider it. The state censors of Pennsylvania thought it impaired morals to refer to approaching maternity. Several years ago the New York Society for the Suppression of Vice brought a book salesman into court for selling a copy of "Mademoiselle De Maupassant." The case was dismissed and the salesman sued the society for damages done to his reputation. In order that the jury might properly estimate the wickedness of this French classic, counsel was permitted to read the book aloud line for line, while judge, jury and lawyers followed the story. The injured salesman was victorious, the jury awarding him generous damages.

But I am sure that lawyer might have so read his text, relocating his points of emphasis, as to create in the minds of the jury a different impression. If evil reactions are due not wholly to intrinsic qualities in a book or play, but to extrinsic conditions, how is a censor to determine before a production what censoring is best for the community and for the free development of art?

We particularly like Mr. Heywood Broun's suggestion that censors ought to bar plays because they are bad art rather than bad morals. He defends his proposition on the ground that one is just as much a matter of opinion as the other. The amusing thing about this question of immoral plays is that a play which is moral enough on Broadway might not be permitted on the lower east side. It is possible for *Life* to print without reproach an anecdote that would take on new color in the pages of the *Police Gazette*. The best way to censor our plays would be to censor the audiences. We wonder whether the respectable theater-going public, which passes by the local burlesque show with coldly averted shoulder, is aware that through all of these years of increasing freedom from the restraint of dress upon the stage, the Columbia Theater, parent of burlesque shows, never permitted bare legs. Up and down Broadway, while the drama and the hosiery manufacturers were getting further and further apart, one little oasis of morality resisted the encroachments of this desert of crime. A parson from Kankakee could go to the Columbia, alone of all Broadway houses, confident that his morals would be unimpaired by the sight of too much girl in the original. And behold, this was the last place on Broadway that anyone would dream

of taking him for the sake of his morals.
Why? Goodness knows. What is goodness?
We are trying hard to find out, but it cannot
be defined by a politically appointed board
of censors.

I do not want a politically appointed censor,
however conscientious he may be, to super-
vise the writing of this article. The very
thought of him led me to tread softly when I
wrote of inciting to violence. I might quote
Samuel Adams, as his words still stand in
the organic law of Massachusetts, and the
National Security League would have me
arrested. I might quote the Bible, and be
suppressed by the Anti-Vice Society. Mind
you, the National Security League might
benefit society by suppressing me, and the
Anti-Vice Society might properly restrain
indiscriminate quoting of the wrong parts
of the Bible. The trouble is, they have got
to know my motives if they are to under-
take censorship, because my motive is sure
to shine through the surface of my committed
act, and modify or intensify its effect upon
men.

The one conclusion which I find looming
more and more inevitably in my mind is that
the millennium will not be possible until each

individual becomes the responsible guardian of his own self—motives, acts, and all; and that, although it may seem a good thing for society, in its present state of sin, for organizations to spring into being that are pledged to mind the manners and preferences of other people, it would be an even better thing for society for a large organization to become incorporated wherein every individual earnestly pledged himself to mind his own manners. One man governing himself well is a better thing for the community than one man governing another.

THAT ELUSIVE WEST

A BORN New Yorker has gotten over his provincialism when he stops thinking of Chicago as a part of "The West." Just when a born Bostonian gets over his I have no means of knowing. Not long ago a Boston lady remarked regretfully, "My son has spent so many of his formative years outside of Boston that he is really quite provincial"; and only the other day a Harvard professor wrote me expressing regret that my town of Poughkeepsie, somewhere to the west of him, is "not on any main line of travel." I do not insist that a Harvard professor shall know where Poughkeepsie is; I am satisfied if he can spell it. But this distinguished scholar knew—and regretted for my sake, I presume—that it was not touched by any of the great trunk lines, namely, the New York, New Haven & Hartford and the Bangor & Aroostook.

Though New England born and New York

broken, it has been my good fortune to live
in Chicago, and visit from Kansas City to
Texas and the coast, so in my effort to locate
"the West," certain preliminary surveys already had their bench marks in my mind.
I knew already that Chicago and Kansas
City are "East." St. Louis I knew enough
about to put in a category by itself. So
much of southern blood is there, and so much
of personality appertains to it as the old-
time fur market for the trapping frontier,
that even a Nevada man does not identify
it as wholly eastern. But such little conti-
nental exploration as I had already done
left me still possessed of a vague uncertainty
as to the whereabouts of the West. In
common with every other properly nurtured
eastern youth, the West meant to me in my
boyhood something beside a region geograph-
ically located. It meant a realm spiritual
as well as physical. Indians in war-paint
had been there recently, cowboys and horses
must be there still, with vast open spaces of
mountain or plain; also the primitive virtues
must obtrude themselves, standing out in
high relief like the morals in old-fashioned
Sunday-school books; and above all a certain
indefinable *informality* must exist—legal, po-

litical, social—with a lack of self-consciousness regarding it.

Age destroys many illusions, and I grew
to know that old-fashioned bad men were
almost nowhere outside the movies, while
small motor cars made in Detroit were
probably everywhere. Yet still I have cher-
ished a dream of a West that I should at once
recognize wherever I found it, rejecting
spurious imitations however far across the
Mississippi they might be.

There is a poem which has wide currency
just now in the geographical West. It is
entitled, "Out where the West begins," and
it is most monopolizing in its claim upon the
simpler and humbler human virtues. "Out
where the handclasp's a little stronger, out
where the smile dwells a little longer"—I
do not blame any geographical westerner for
liking it. It is a good poem. But I distrust one who pins it on his sitting room wall.
It lends itself dangerously to parody. Some
coarse fellow will write a stanza entitled
"Out where the chest begins," and I for one
shall greatly deplore it. But if I used that
poem for a guide, I might easily wander
anywhere, away from the selfishness bred of
crowded life into some remote Vermont or

Virginia homestead, or to any quiet country-
side where folk are dependent upon all of the
humbler virtues to make their world go
round, and most people are hospitable without talking about it.

Columbus believed that by traveling west
one may attain the east. That old-timer was
right in my opinion, for the West of my
dream lies not on the Pacific slope. Different
that coast is, and admirable, of course, but
its sins and its virtues seem to me those of
my own section, with a local twist to them.
And surely one landmark by which I sought
to recognize my promised land is conspic-
uously missing—that certain lack of self-
consciousness. My West might be boast-
ful, aggressive, self-confident—with the perfect assurance of healthy youth—but not
forever self-conscious. The former smacks
of ingenuousness, the latter of sophistica-
tion. The Coast is sophisticated.

I do not mean this for disparagement.
If an easterner dares to disparage the merits
of California, a Californian need call up only
one retort: "Why, then, are we overrun by
easterners, immigrant and transient?" I suspect one could travel farther in certain parts
of New York state without meeting a New

Yorker than he could in most of California.
Over-production in Detroit is partly responsible for that. But my West evidently
must lie somewhere between the center of
population and the coast. No one can guide
me to a dream's realization; it is my own
dream. I alone am the old nurse who can
recognize the strawberry mark on the left
shoulder of the missing heir.

A line drawn through the Dakotas, Nebraska, Kansas, and Oklahoma marks where
the geographical West begins. It seemed reasonable to try to pick up the trail there. It
is one of the perquisites of professoring that
one may sometimes travel far afield on a
small income, borrowing a leaf from Tommy
Tucker's book. In Nebraska I chanced upon
a town which boasts that it is equidistant to
a mile from Boston and from San Francisco.
Perhaps there is legitimate pleasure in the
thought that you are just as far from one
as from the other. The West, they say,
is given to bragging. This reminds me
that I met a man there who by every
claim of blood and heritage belongs to the
Hub, but he is living somewhere in the neighborhood of the periphery. He told me that
old Cambridge associates of his had asked

him why he did not come back and settle
down in Boston. "I should like to," he
said, "if it were not for the fact that Boston
is so far away."

"Far from what?" said they, aghast.

"So far away from Denver," he answered
placidly. He told me that thereupon the
conversation ended abruptly.

This little city that I found in Nebraska
was not my West, but I made the hopeful
discovery that it was a boom town. Visions
of Virginia City came to mind, and Poker
Flat and Roaring Camp. Here in Nebraska,
however, was not a boom of discovered oil or
precious metal, but of a more eastern thing.
It was the attempt to realize an extravagant
manufacturing dream on the part of certain
financiers. Broad avenues were laid out.
There was a trolley before there were passen-
gers. Great mills were planned, and one was
constructed before there were any available
operatives for the looms. Then, in Through-
the-Looking-Glass fashion, the population began to come and the town to grow up within
the shell of it. Suddenly something financial
collapsed, and the new population stopped
coming and some of those who were there
went away. And now, slowly, upon the

foundation of crumbling hopes, a solid, more normally established community is growing. They have the legacy of broad avenues, and the western realization that there is room in the world for building; so there is less scrimping and crowding together of even the humblest homes.

Nebraska is a vast garden; one travels interminably through fields of grain, apparently without a fallow acre between the holdings. And I find here evidences of certain mental attitudes distinctly uneastern, where the people themselves think of the East as though it were a different and remote section. This alone would seem to indicate that they themselves must belong to another province. What is the cause of this certain sensitiveness toward "eastern" opinion? It must be merely a repetition of that old chip-on-the-shoulder attitude of dwellers on our eastern seaboard toward visitors from effete Europe. This is no subtle imagination of mine. Time and again a host or hostess has said, "You must find us very crude out here." The statement is always a form of question, and in a tone of voice that varies with the temperament of the questioner from deprecatory to bellicose. Honest, unaffected simpli-

city, which is what one most often finds, is
a different thing from crudeness, but the
very effort to answer such a question is a
cause for embarrassment and stumbling of
speech.

Kansas is equally centered, but my first
glimpse of Kansas after getting well beyond
the river boded ill in its physical appearance
for the finding of my promised land. From
the railroad station in another little city, I
drove in a taxi up a narrow elm-shaded street
past New England door-yards. The great
branches actually interlaced above my head.
The houses, with green blinds and inviting
porches, cried aloud to me that I had strayed
into the Berkshires. Truly, one gets east
by going west. Those early settlers who
went out from New England on a crusade
into bleeding Kansas crawled across the
country like snails, in their day of inadequate
transportation, and like snails, too, they must
have carried their houses upon their backs.
No town in Massachusetts is any more like
old New England than is this town in middle-
eastern Kansas.

But since my West is partly a thing of the
spirit, I must stop looking too sharply at the
physical outlines. Yes, here in Kansas and

Oklahoma, and to some extent in Nebraska, there is something new and strange in the attitude of the people, or let me say strange rather than new. One will find among the hills of New England and of the South fragments of pure English speech that have died out of old England. So it is possible that some of these spiritual characteristics of this land where the West begins are characteristics of Americanism as it was in the East when the East was younger. Some of it I liked and some of it I didn't, and that which I disliked I was a bit ashamed of myself for disliking, as though I found that I had grown cynical and veneered with an unworthy cosmopolitanism. No man, for instance, can go up and down through Oklahoma and Kansas and Nebraska, and assert that the eighteenth amendment and the Volstead act were forced upon our statute books by a vociferous minority. A referendum would find opposition to these laws throughout this territory so relatively small as to destroy forever the hopes of their enemies on the two seaboards.

People go to church to-day out there in the midland as they used to go in New England, with sectarianism still rampant. A kindly old gentleman who was my host in one of these midway states catechized me. "I hear," he said, "that denominationalism in the East is not as strong as it used to be."

I agreed cheerfully that I guessed that was so.

"It is too bad," he said gravely. "It means that some of the vigor is gone from their religious belief." Then he proceeded by tactful questions to locate if possible my own denominational anchorage. I evaded the issue, for reasons that need not be discussed. He was courteous, and soon desisted. I think he concluded in his kind-heartedness that I belonged to some sect so poorly represented in his state that I was embarrassed to mention it. "Ah, well," he said, in a most conciliatory way, "after all, all Christians are brothers, and you can divide them up into two great groups—those that believe in immersion and those that don't." I nodded my head wisely, and turned the conversation into the field of politics.

In a certain one of these states there are the makings of a really great state university. All the auspices are in its favor, save a suspicion throughout some of the country-side that it may not be evangelically orthodox.

Religious denominations have built their own dormitories upon the campus, in order to keep a closer watch over their own boys and girls; and only a few miles away one denomination hopes for a competing university of its own, at a cost of millions to be raised largely within the state, so that its own young people need not go to an undenominational institution.

The small endowed colleges are not unknown throughout these western states. Like most eastern endowed institutions, they were all established by religious sects, in many cases before the state university came into existence; but unlike their eastern sisters, they hold strictly to their first anchorage. And they perform an unexpected function in that they provide education at a lower cost than it can generally be had at the overshadowing state university where tuition itself is free.

It is probably true that where there is greater narrowness of belief there is more of what Mayor Gaynor termed "outward appearance of decency." You see, I am trying to protect myself against the statement that this midland country is cleaner than the East. At least it acts cleaner. If I have not yet found even the beginning of my West, I am sure that I have left my East. These great schools and universities that I have glimpsed along my trail are different, utterly different. They are educating youth just as it comes by the wholesale, and adjusting their standards to that need. Some of them suffer from what I have called "educational elephantiasis"; and certain weaknesses that seem to come with bigness I have dared to hint at, elsewhere. But I admit the presumption of any supercilious critic, trained in an old endowed institution of the Altantic seaboard, who attempts to estimate the work of some of these institutions in terms of his own experience. They have selected certain problems to face, and they are new problems. How can one best administer the educational funds of a commonwealth in order to educate the largest possible number of that commonwealth's citizenry? The young first, of course, because they are more educatable. But the old as well—anyone and every one. It is easy to complain that the methods and even the standards of the University of Calisota differ from those of Princeton. It is also possible to say that the methods and standards of Princeton differ from those of

Calisota. Boston is as far from Denver as
Denver is from Boston. But the interesting
fact is that here are new problems and large
problems, and they are being faced in new,
large ways. Leaders are handicapped by the
miserable pettiness of state politics, but no
one will maintain that that is a phenomenon
peculiar to the West. In the summer school
of one of these midland state universities I
find more than a thousand students at work,
mostly state teachers working to improve
their chances for promotion. But scattered
through those student ranks I find mothers
who have brought their babies with them,
fathers who have to get back to the farm at
intervals, or even every day, sometimes two
generations in the same family working side by
side. The sight cannot fail to inspire one.
Then, to my astonishment, only twenty or
thirty miles away, I find a normal school with
its summer quota of about two thousand, all
at work. I learn that in Nebraska alone there
are ten great summer schools in action, in-
cluding the one at the University; over the
state line, in Kansas, there are eight more;
and over in Oklahoma, eight more. University
extension courses and "Chautauqua" lectures
are reaching further still. I am beginning to

get a sense of the largeness of things, and of the problems that accompany bigness, and I say to myself, "I am on the edge of my West."

Something else dominantly wins my attention here in Kansas, due doubtless to personal predilection. I am trying to read as I run, and I read some comfort to my soul out of the Kansas press. It is easy to become depressed over the state of American newspapers, and to lose that depression in Kansas. The sense of personal responsibility for the behavior of a personally owned and edited newspaper still exists here. The Atchison *Globe*, the Emporia *Gazette*, and a dozen others less well known, are published in towns of twelve or thirteen thousand population each. The Topeka *Capitol* is issued in a city of fifty thousand. Yet they guide the opinions of a public spread over wide areas, and their judgments are quoted from ocean to ocean. They are institutions of dignity and power. Contemporaries in many a city of greater size in other sections of the country bristle with fraudulent advertising and serve up carelessly garnered news and dish-water editorials. I find an editor-owner of one of these small papers sitting in his first-floor sanctum with its bay window looking out

upon the street; greeted by all and sundry
as they pass, accessible to all; and meeting
to the full his share of the obligations of a
free press in a democracy. Here are some of
the primitive virtues, and some of the infor-
malities, and a certain lack of self-consciousness; let a cynic find what he may on the
reverse of the shield. I think a breeze is
blowing strongly on me out of my "West."

Once again one attains the East by traveling westward. Over the line in Colorado,
on the eastern slope, one meets the tourist
rampant. Motor cars pause by the roadside
and indecently deliver themselves of canvas
tents and cots and bedding, and people camp
there, and their voices are voices of the East.
Vast hotels offer all the conveniences of At-
lantic City, with a mountain panorama from
the front piazzas substituted for a seascape.
Yet there are wide spaces, Indian curios are
for sale, and great saddles with horns upon
them. I must be headed right! Tourists
climbing mountains or motoring toward "dude
ranches" in Wyoming obscure my trail.
Beyond the passes I become more confident.
One may buy a burro (for the price of an
hour's ride in Central Park) and pack through
deserted mining towns, and fish—for fish—

and find mountain views unmarred by a
hotel in the foreground or even a struggling
motor car.

Now I know that I am west because of the
attitude toward me and my tribe. So I am
from the East? They, too, were east once
to visit a grandfather in Ohio, Chicago is
a fine city. From east of Chicago? Oh,
are you? I am talking now of the man in the
grocery store, on the street corner, in the
smoker of the local. Strange, how provincialism still obtains anywhere in the face of a
three-penny press and modern transportation! The man on the smoker is friendly,
with the instinctive tact of his friendliness;
more tactful, in fact, than your eastern
provincial talking to a westerner. But he
distrusts the East. It is the Englishman and
the American of the 'fifties all over again in
a smaller circle. The easterner shows frequently a certain condescension toward west-
erners. The forms taken by this interpro-
vincial distrust are amusingly uniform. Before we entered the war I heard many an
eastern man express the belief that the great
menace to national unity of action was latent
in the West. "They are so wrapped up in
their own selfish affairs—the war doesn't

touch them except to make money for them."
The western provincial, aroused to the need
for war, said over and over on his street
corners, "The threat against national unity
of action is in the East. They're too busy
making money. But we can do the job
without them." To-day I find my western
friend in the smoker concerned over the dena-
tionalization of the East, because of its surrender to socialism, bolshevism, capitalism,
and every *ism* save patriotism; and at once
I recall the serious concern of my eastern
friends over farmer coöperative movements
in the Northwest and any sort of legislation
in Kansas. I am afraid the great power of
the press, instead of bringing us together,
sometimes helps to keep us apart, by making
mountains of molehills and forest fires of
burning refuse. Yet it was not a three penny
western press, but a commercially minded
eastern periodical with a large western circulation, that recently capitalized this provincialism by making silly charges of disloyalty
against a whole group of eastern colleges.

I am finding myself in a different section of
country, even in my rôle of Tommy Tucker.
Here is a music teacher leaving his work for
a more lucrative position "in the East"—

perhaps in Michigan or Wisconsin. I congratulate him. "Yes," he answers, "it's a promotion, of course, but I'll never get such stimulating pupils again. They must have all I've got. Pupils have come to me here bringing diplomas to prove that they have had a full correspondence course in piano playing, and they have *never touched a piano in their lives*. But they mean business so intensely that even such poor means have enabled them to master some of the theory and I can carry them so much the farther in my work because of it."

But in my search I find that this great West is made up of many lesser wests. I am astonished at a Texan student's indignation because I thought his twist of speech like that of a man from Arkansas. I am surprised until I recall my first experience with a group of San Franciscans all simultaneously praising California—until I mentioned Los Angeles. Wide geographical horizons are no cure for provincialism. I have met a New York farmer who distrusted anyone born the other side of Lake Champlain, and a Maine woodsman with a sense of kinship to human kind as all-inclusive as St. Peter's.

Ask a Colorado tourist for the highest mountain in the state and he will cry, "Pike's Peak," and tell you there is a cog-rail and a fine motor road to the top. But it was toward Mt. Blanca, well to the south of the greatest tourist activity, that my trail led me. A mountain is in some ways as high as it looks. Yet when I have scaled a summit it is more interesting to know how far I am above the level I started from, than above some ocean I cannot see. For the same natural reason the Holyoke hills in the Connecticut valley proclaim themselves far more dramatically than does much of the coast range in California. But Blanca is not only the highest summit in Colorado—it looks and acts highest. It rears its great bulk up from the plain in a majestic loneliness, robed in ever-changing cloud garments and crowned with snow. Southward from it runs the Sangre de Cristo range of the Rockies, far down into New Mexico. The first glimpse of that range was a hint of my promised land. The San Luis valley, blocked at the north by Blanca, extends its fertile length for sixty miles or so, and merges with the valley of the Rio Grande—ending far to the south near Santa Fé. The eastward wall for the entire

two hundred miles of that fertile ranch-
dotted ribbon is the Sangre de Cristo—
rising abruptly from the plain to summits
above timber line. Deep and narrow cañons
cut into it at intervals—the final retreat of
that romantic race, the old-fashioned bad
men of blessed dime novel memory. Here is
the final frontier! Home seekers are in the
valley, but few tourists have found it, save at
Taos, where a group of artists threaten now
by their brushes to tell the world. Within
their small radius livery rates mount rapidly
and Indians take to posing and forsake agriculture.

From the summit of Lobo, ten thousand
feet up in that glorious brotherhood of summits, I looked out upon my promised land.
I had sought great open spaces: below me
lay the valley of the Rio Grande—in reality
a plateau seventy-five miles wide bisected by
a thread of brown that I knew to be the river
cañon five hundred feet deep. Far away to
the westward, clearly defined in the clear air,
were other summits parallel to mine—the
great divide. Somewhere far down below
on my mountain side, but seven thousand
feet above the level of some ocean somewhere
—God rest its soul—is a log cabin with a

doorway commanding more sunset than I thought the sky could hold. The nearest railroad is forty miles away. A doctor? There is one at Taos. Sheridan once rode the same distance hurriedly in an emergency. Why worry about a doctor? The nearest chiropodist is in Santa Fé and there isn't a delicatessen this side of Denver. One learns to adapt oneself.

Indians? Ask the artists of Taos. There never were such Indians in the most fanciful story book. Tall, sedate, oriental, garbed in white, as they were when the Spaniards found them; living still in their great pueblo on land the Spaniards respected four hundred years ago—truly I have my Indians.

Does anyone ever realize a dream to the full? I am trying to recall my specifications, as I sit here on the edge of a stream in a deep cañon whose walls are painted red and gray and green with clay soil and sage-brush and piñon trees. A few hundred yards away, half hidden by a projecting cliff, are the picturesque ruins of Turley's mill, unaltered by the hand of man since the day when Indians and Mexicans laid siege there and finally captured and massacred all of the inmates. The traditions of the country-side are all picturesque and stimulating to the imagination. Turley was avenged, as was the murdered governor of the state, by a little body of soldiers who marched a hundred miles through a hostile country over trails that seem impossible to-day, dragging a small howitzer. They captured the Indian pueblo, hurling explosive ammunition by hand through the windows of the fortified church. It was such grenade action as had never occurred before or since, until the great war. The record of our little American army before its expansion teems with such dramatic episodes; and the memory of them, and the ghosts of such uncanonized heroes, help to make my West.

Yesterday evening after dark two cattle men of the old school tied their horses to the corral gate and came in to take pot-luck with us. They had left their cattle in the cañon, and were riding home. "It isn't the country it was," said one of them. (Strange, how we always bemoan the fading glories of the past, even while coyotes yap out of the darkness beyond the corral!) "Taos is full of tourists—I saw two there yesterday—and the Indians are posing too much for their pictures. I've had some good times in that old town. I remember when a couple of Mormons brought a fast horse down there to race him against all comers. The Indians over to the pueblo had a pretty good trotter of their own, so they accepted the challenge. The Mormons were working their horse every day, getting him ready, so the Indians went in one night and stole him and tried him out against their own, back of the pueblo. They found out theirs was faster, so they bet everything they had—blankets, moccasins, money, crops, everything. All this betting worried the Mormons, so they brought in a professional jockey. The Indians then shipped in one for themselves from Denver or somewhere. The day before the race the Indians got an idea the Mormons had tampered with the Denver jockey, so they had a little conference with him and told him that three of the best marksmen of the tribe were sitting behind some sage-brush near the home stretch armed with Winchesters, and that if he didn't come in ahead they were going to shoot him off the horse. That was the greatest race I ever saw," said our guest. "The Indians' jockey won by a neck, with his head craned around over his shoulder and his eyes fixed on those sage bushes, and that night the

Indians had the biggest party that ever was held in these parts, with everybody welcome."

One doesn't need to believe everything a cowboy tells. All one asks is that the cowboy shall continue telling.

What else did I say that I wanted? Was it horses? They are cheaper to buy than to hire, and one of their uses is to pull an occasional stray touring car out of a hole in the road. They are little beasts, inclined to boniness, particularly if a Mexican has owned them. Every properly reared American small boy knows the kind. He calls it a "cayuse" or a "bronc," and he talks to it in companionable fashion as he gallops around the back yard, oblivious to the fact that in this instance it closely resembles a broomstick. Except for the ponies of the Indians, which have been reared by them through generations past, these range horses are an unpedigreed lot, and would present a sorry, or at least a dejected, appearance in an eastern horse show. But who wouldn't? Their chief development is in the brain. They tease for salt, knocking with a front hoof upon the cabin steps, nuzzle against you as they plead for oats or ask to be scratched, and then nip a piece out of you if you draw the cinch too tight. They are as moody as a prima donna, one day coming at your call, and the next day leading you an hour's chase around the pasture, or hiding behind brushwood to escape your notice. There are two sorrels resting up in the field with the pigs. The other day the most terrific squawling assailed our ears from the direction of the sty. Going to investigate, I found that an old porker had thrust his nose through the narrow wire mesh of the fence in some fit of curiosity and his two protruding tusks had hooked over the wires one on either side and held him there. The more he pulled the worse it hurt him, and the noise was terrific. Grouped back of him were some of his relatives, evidently much excited, but at his side, bending over him, was one of the sorrels, licking his ear in a perfectly obvious effort to show sympathy. When I was a small boy on a ranch in old Mexico, with a chance to ride behind the cattle, I remember that I hesitatingly asked for instructions in the game. The chief laughed. "I have given you a good cow pony," he said. "He knows more about herding cattle than you'll ever learn. He may teach you some of it, but he won't let you ride him wrong."

Cowboys, Indians in the flesh, the memories of old raids and the ghosts of old raiders, and—what else was it? Those qualities of the spirit—a pervading informality and a lack of self-consciousness regarding it! This is not the Southwest that I am in. The Southwest means to me the alkali plains and cactus, the Grand Cañon and buttes and mesas. This is north of all that—wonderfully forested. Yet nine-tenths of the people are Mexican, gentle, friendly, inconsequent, and the scattering of Anglo Saxons are all the closer, kindlier neighbors for the reason of their scarcity. Informality—legal, political, social—it is all here. The self-assurance of the true West is in the tones and conversation throughout these settlements on the western slope and southward. No one asks whether an easterner "thinks us crude." Nobody cares what an easterner thinks. East is out of their world, existing only in the newspapers, a land of doubtful ideals and questionable morals.

"Can you advise me about a school for my daughter?" says a chance acquaintance. "Missouri? I have thought of Missouri, but I don't want to send her East. A girl isn't safe there. What do you know about Colo-

rado and New Mexico schools?" By schools
he meant anything from a boarding school
to a university.

A most notable characteristic of my West
is its power of assimilation. Let a man
from Ohio or Idaho or Kentucky move to
New York, and he is always ready to plead
not guilty to New York birth, unless he
becomes one of the negligible members of
that circle once termed the four hundred.
He is forever attending his annual state
dinners, and contributing to charities and
other community enterprises "back home."
My West assimilates its immigrants in a
month; in a year they pretend they are first
settlers. Even back in Oklahoma, that state
which is neither north nor south, but a product of all sections and all the world, I visit a
town where unwritten law says that no negro
shall be found within the city limits after six
P. M., and the most earnest advocate of "this
policy of ours," as he explains to me its
causes and its beneficial results, is a man not
so many months away from Cambridge,
Massachusetts.

Social informality and quick assimilation
must be inevitable where the community is
young and healthy, and lacking in a morbid

self-consciousness. My westerner thinks of every man as a neighbor and a friend until the contrary has been proved, and usually addresses him as such. Your easterner follows the reverse method. O. Henry has it right in his story of the westerner who roamed New York with a growing feeling of intense loneliness, addressing strangers and receiving cold stares in return. Finally he went back to a certain cafe where the manager had volunteered the remark, "Nice day." He found his man again, displayed a loaded gun, and demanded further remarks about the weather, as well as some conversation about the wife and kids.

The worst thing for my West-of-the-spirit is easterners who refuse to be assimilated. Most tourists are such, of course. Tactless curiosity must in the long run produce morbid self-consciousness. Coldness and unfriendliness must eventually force a like response. The East could produce no more pathetic spectacle than I saw in the smoking compartment of a west-bound Pullman out of Denver. A cow puncher, riding home in luxury after superintending a sale of cattle, was regaling a group of eastern tourists with cheap and profane stories of his own marvelous prowess.

He had been to the movies night after night, and had discovered what a cowboy ought to be in the eyes of easterners.

I am sitting on the edge of a stream in the cañon. If the trout are biting to-day, surely they must, as the small boy complained, be biting each other, for they certainly have paid no attention to my casting. But what do I care? I have found my West.

"Goliath was a Philistine who had grown too fast. I wouldn't mind how big I was, if I had a proportionate amount of horse-sense."

—EPHRAIM STEBBINS.

ELEFANTASIES

STRIVING for mere bulk is a national pastime that we like to think we have outgrown. Even a citizen of Chicago hesitates nowadays and glances furtively about before he taps his vis-à-vis impressively upon the waistcoat button and says, "Chicago has the longest street in the world. More cattle are slaughtered in our city in one week than die in a decade in Cathay." This type of confidence was once a cause of widespread complaint against the average Chicagoan, until he outgrew it. Chicago had begun to develop in ways other than physical. Later on, the center of superlatives moved to St. Louis, and then to Kansas City. Not long ago it was located, we believe, in the geographical center of San Francisco bay, with a strong pull to the southward from Los Angeles, which promised soon to draw it away altogether.

We are willing to admit that in Dickens's

day Americans were constantly bragging of
mere size. Yet this, oddly enough, did not
necessarily prove us braggarts at heart; rather
was it a superficiality, a shell that covered
souls sensitively conscious of shortcomings.
In the crudest 'fifties any average American
recognized that there were great national de-
ficiencies in the realm of culture. He felt that
they must be at once apparent to a visitor
from the more highly refined civilizations of
Europe, and he hastened, like a cuttlefish, to
throw out a smoke-screen of superlatives, to
protect the national reputation from attack.

That day has passed. American art and
letters, and other refinements of civilization,
have been superimposed upon the sturdy
physical structure that was once our only and
our true boast. Nowadays we dare address
the visiting foreigner even in deprecatory
terms, confident that he will find here without
our guidance qualities of many sorts comparable to those of his own native land.

This is true of the country as a whole. The
center of braggadocio has moved so far west
that it should rightfully have disappeared long
ago into the Pacific, and be now reappearing
among the oriental islands. But from time to
time we are made aware by a newspaper clip-

ping or a bit of conversation that the boast of bulk is still voiced in some retarded section of our country as a proof of final attainment. Does it at last prove the true braggart, or is it still camouflage—a pose to cover the fact that sensitive souls recognize their community to be deficient in the finer things?

The longest street in the world, the biggest tree, the largest strawberry, are themselves no detriment to a community, unless they actually crowd out justifications for a finer sort of superlative. Even the spiritually minded must take a sneaking sort of pride in mere size. Jumbo was indeed an admirable elephant! But it would be a serious matter if this admiration for bulk set an entire community upon the wrong track, because of the grotesque notion that quantity proves quality.

Not long ago I had a strange dream. It seemed to me that in some state or other, rumor was running like a prairie fire that with a little effort the state university might become the largest seat of higher education in the land. Here was a superlative almost within reach, compared to which bulk in trees and fruits and other material things sank into insignificance. For would not bulk in an educational institution prove bulk in mental attainment as well, so that two superlatives could be caught in one trap? So I dreamed that the directorate of the university, backed by loyal sons of the commonwealth, reached out eagerly for students.

It has been frequently noted how easily the mental balance of a sane individual may be lost in the emotion of a crowd—clergymen in the 'fifties defending slavery, scholars in Germany rejoicing over the *Lusitania*. So we can imagine (if my dream were true) how honest and scholarly reasoners, surrounded by popular clamor for bulk, would discover that bulk itself actually served the purposes of scholarship, or at least of education. So it proved in my dream. Scholars in plenty connected with the institution suddenly discovered that all education in a democracy must be within immediate reach of all— higher education no less than lower. It is the duty of a state university, they said, to be available to every boy and girl in the state who has finished high school, and to make itself as easy of attainment as possible. The matter of educational standard may be considered after admission, but first of all it is imperative that all who wish should be admitted. Only thus may the function of the state university be carried out. Others reasoned that if bulk was the one argument that the state legislature could understand, then let the university first acquire numbers, at any cost.

So I dreamed that throughout the state every high school was empowered to certify its graduates for admission to the university without examination; and though a few concientious high school principals at first required some standard of attainment before granting a certificate, standing alone in such a quixotic position soon proved too great an effort, and in time certificates were cheapened equally from one end of the state to the other. Then—glorious news!—rumor ran from mouth to mouth that the state university had a larger enrollment than any other institution of its kind in the world, and loyal citizens leaned back in their chairs and beamed with satisfaction over this final proof of their beloved state's preëminence, now at last in the field of mental attainment.

Let us be grateful that all this was a dream! But it might be interesting to consider what would happen to a university attempting to digest such a mortal gorge. In the first place, the usual percentage of students attending

the university for no reasons other than social
would be greatly increased. Boys and girls
with no educational aim whatever would
tend to lower the standards of those classrooms which largely received their patronage.
Moreover, a state university dependent upon
legislative action for funds could not respond
at once to demands for more instruction.
Budgets are fixed for a certain time ahead.
A thousand students selecting a course in
economics might find salaried instructors
sufficient only for five hundred students.
Every possible stretching of the exchequer
by the authorities could not provide fit men
and women to meet this need during the
current year, and students would find themselves under fellow students of honor grade,
rather than receiving the benefit of mature
instruction. A hundred students, it is safe
to guess, might find themselves in a "Spoken
French" classroom attempting to master
French conversation by a fifty-minute asso-
ciation three times a week with one harassed
French expert. Students of weaker moral
resistance might find themselves over-tempted
to plan absences from overcrowded classrooms unbeknown to the instructor. The
same type of students might the more easily

substitute for one another. Such crimes have been known. I recall now that in my dream there was an instance of a student receiving a high mark in a course that he had not attended at all, and two freshmen electing Sanskrit under the vague impression that it was a science, perhaps having something to do with a sand-box, but content to know that it came at an hour which fitted in with their social engagements.

In other words, such an educational structure might collapse of its own weight. Those earnest apologists for no sifting process at entrance would discover that because of resultant circumstances the establishment of a standard among these hordes after entrance was enormously difficult, and such a standard of higher education as we should like to have maintained somewhere in America quite impossible.

This was indeed a gloomy elefantasm. I make no defense for it, other than to claim that it presents a picture of something which might occur, here or there in our broad land. Assume that such a case of educational elephantiasis were to develop. What is the cure? Surely a vast number of American boys and girls brought together in the name of higher education, in an environment adapted to its pursuit, is an inspiring thought, even though a foolish striving for mere bulk aided their assemblage. Perhaps the establishment of certain recognized educational standards among them would be impossible. Then, perhaps, in such an institution it would be better to face that fact and establish new ones.

Is a little education for everybody better than a great deal of education for a few? Such a question is not a fair one. The two things are not mutually exclusive. No one, to whom the picture is new, can fail to be thrilled by the sight of thousands of young people brought together in one beautiful spot in the pursuit of learning. But surely there is still an aristocracy of education that will exist, whatever powers arise to crush it, and however for a time they may succeed. And it is doubtful whether any public can lift itself by its boot-straps. Yet—a little more education for everybody!—that must be worth while. If a vast undergraduate university might arise which would frankly admit such to be its whole purpose, and not claim for its baccalaureate degree an exact parity with the degree awarded by educational machines operated in a different fashion, full justification might well be acknowledged by the entire fraternity of scholars.

Some time ago, a Columbia University professor stated that in his opinion the day of great educational segregation was at hand. The accumulation of wealth and power at these centers would make it impossible for small colleges to continue and to justify their own existence. Yet within a year of that statement, progressive administrators in more than one great institution were discussing the advantages of some sort of unscrambling operation, and the establishment of many distinct small colleges of liberal arts, under a system similar to that of English universities. Some of these administrators are now for reaching out and gathering under their wings all detached small colleges in the state. Whether or not the motive is wholly altruistic I cannot say.

A few years ago I attended a banquet to celebrate a new development in paper bag cookery. After a delicious meal, various speakers arose to sing its praises, among them Mr. Gelett Burgess. In the course of his remarks he praised the dinner, expressed his approval of the method, but suggested that there were one or two obvious disadvantages to the little bags which had appeared upon our plates. In the first place, they were difficult to handle. He suggested that in the future various improvements upon the idea might appear. The bags, for greater convenience, would be made of some rigid material; then, because of the difficulty of entering them, one side would be left open; then eventually, for convenience of manipulation, some inventive genius would attach a handle; and he could prophetically see, in the far distant future, the gradual evolving of the saucepan.

A most interesting phenomenon in our American world of education is the occasional seismic disturbance, with its resultant ripple upon the waters, when the president of some large university rediscovers the small college.

A short time ago, a small New England college, which considers limiting its numbers to six hundred students, announced such an increase in faculty salaries and such a rigid maintenance of standards as would enable it to compete with any university when seeking teachers of the best sort. It also promised to every professor of science a private laboratory for research, with assistants to aid in the caring for apparatus, and others to aid with instruction. In this particular small college there is at present one teacher to every ten students. Moreover, eighty-four per cent of the faculty are of professorial rank. These facts, interpreted, amount to just this: that students are permitted to come into direct relationship with the best teachers of the institution, and the college is able to secure men of the best sort. In contrast, a great university in the east offers to its undergraduates in liberal arts one teacher to every twenty-two students, and a faculty only sixty per cent of professorial rank. There are other great universities with a larger percentage of new-fledged instructors, offering undergraduate instruction to over-large groups of young men nearly as old as themselves.

Now and then one sees in display type the statement that such and such a department store is the largest in the state or in the Chattahoochee Valley. Fortunate is the town that boasts a commercial enterprise that has grown to these proportions. Such a store is able to go far afield in its search for goods and bring new satisfactions to its customers. Beside its power to serve in reducing middlemen's profits it may be an actual means of education within a wide circumference of outlying farms and scattered houses.

But there is a small inscription on the other side of the shield. This great concern establishes a book department, let us say. Since its policy is to handle in quantity it can afford to carry only "sure sellers"—widely advertised fiction and certain essential household books and standard reprints. It cannot train or even afford the book-loving expert behind the counter, but must often find its salesman by promotion from hardware or toilet goods. Books are just another wholly material commodity. Sometimes they are sold at cost to lure customers. Well, why not?

In the same community is a small bookstore which if successful has the power to perform a definite social service all its own, second to that of the town library. Trained clerks advise buyers, reveal literary treasures, talk "shop," and encourage browsing. Yet that bookstore needs the profits from the cheap reprints, the sets, the assured sellers, in order to live, and these the department store takes from it, and it dies. If the publishers find only such quantity distributors for their output it becomes a greater risk to publish the more delicate wares, and a higher price must be charged for them. I have cited elsewhere the claim that there are fewer bookshops to-day in the United States than at the time of the Civil War. If so, the country is the loser. Popular desire is not at fault, but distributing conditions.

Big fruit often lacks flavor. Biggest stores, biggest universities, biggest cities must pay something for their size. Bigness brings about certain ills as well as certain advantages. Perhaps the anti-fat advertisements that are forever affronting the eye convey in their physically intimate phrases a larger moral than their readers or their writers generally discern.

THE DEAD HAND

SOME years ago I visited a most inspiring small college situated in a farming country in the middle west, many miles distant from any large city. It was inspiring because it seemed to be serving the cause of education in that old, self-denying fashion character-istic of the early days of the pioneers. The college of my own undergraduate days, in-creasingly dear to me with the passage of the years, could hardly be said to serve in equal fashion, because in crowded New England one might wipe out an ancient seat of learning with all of its splendid traditions and its notable record, and future students would find some other dame near by to adopt for an *alma mater*. But this school among the grain-fields and orchards lured boys to its classrooms who would not otherwise find any college within their reach. I visited its buildings and walked through its halls, seeing beauties of structure that did not architec-

turally exist, and listening to details from my
kindly guide with a respectful attention that
similar statistics never won from me before.
Then we returned to my host's hospitable
abode for lunch.

"Did you," said my hostess, severely,
"show him the skeleton?"

The professor evaded her question, and
spoke of Latin and Greek, and college loyalty
and athletics.

"Did you," said my hostess, with greater
firmness, "show him the skeleton?"

The professor fidgeted, and we talked of
fraternities and their place in college life.

"If you do not show him the skeleton,"
said my hostess, "I will take him to it myself." And so the story came out.

It seems that many years ago a native
of the community, a man kindly disposed
toward education, perhaps because of his
own lack of it, found himself independently
wealthy and without a purpose in life. He had
read of art-collectors who spent their un-
earned increment upon paintings and works
of sculpture which they assembled into great
collections and eventually donated to some
worthy institution. So he set about the
same thing, and with indefatigable zeal pur-

chased hand-painted pictures from all that countryside—flowers in vases, fishes on dishes, vases and dishes all by themselves or in groups, decorative panels in high colors, all suited to relieve the atmosphere of darkened parlors set with haircloth furniture; even crayon portraits of unlabeled dear ones long since departed. It did not take him long to collect a considerable number, nor did it greatly deplete his fortune, but at last he had an art collection and was in the vogue. When he died he bequeathed a building to the local college, with the stipulation that in that building there should be an art gallery, and that the nucleus of all future art collections should be his own assembled pictures, which he left *in toto* and without further restriction save that they should be perpetually on view.

This was the story. Of course the college accepted the building, conditions and all, and the "closet" which I had not seen was the art-room, and the skeleton in it was that collection.

I should have laughed hilariously had I seen those absurd pictures outside their present environment and without their history; but, as it was, I viewed them unsmiling, for the college seemed to me to have so wonderful a personality and this was such a pathetic episode in its life-story.

I suppose the good man who bequeathed his wealth and his collection had a real desire to be of service, but this desire was somehow bound up with a silly ambition to be classified as one of the famous rich. Many of the teachers in that college, it is safe to say, are living a life of actual self-denial for the sake of service. Art collections and other beautiful things whose value cannot be measured in terms of money are theirs by right, but the hand of this foolish man who died many years ago still offers them a stone.

In the New York Public Library, one of the officials tells me, somewhere among its mysterious hidden passages are various closets locking up skeletons just as strange. People have left bequests, stipulating at the same time that the portrait of the testator's maternal great-aunt shall be permanently and prominently displayed upon the library wall. Often these embarrassing conditions are attached to bequests of great value that could not possibly be refused, and so a dead hand keeps its grip upon some room or some wall space in that great building which so wonderfully serves the people.

I have often wondered what rights the dead have over the living. Some day we shall ask this question of the marble monuments in our great cemeteries, as the city crowds in upon them and the children clamor for breathing-space; but that is a different phase of the problem now in my mind. How much shall the dead be empowered to demand of the living for ancient favors bestowed?

Once upon a time I attended an important ceremony in another of the smaller colleges. A little crowd of young women students were grouped together in one part of the hall, and as I looked at them, after listening to numerous addresses of eulogy and exaltation, it seemed to me that they were an unusually pretty aggregation, and that they themselves were, after all, the finest advertisement of the place, and that all the oratory might just as well have been spared. As I watched the little group it suddenly showed signs of special animation, emitting certain preliminary sounds, as does a clock when about to strike. A cheer-leader stepped out from their midst, and with one united and musical voice they spelled out vociferously, "R-o-b-e-r-t K. J-o-n-e-s! Robert K. Jones!" That

is not really the name they spelled and
shouted so musically, but it is not a whit
longer or more commonplace or unmusical
than the name I am concealing.   So I inquired
about the matter and found that many years
ago one Robert K. Jones had given a com-
paratively small sum of money, as educational bequests go, that he had done it at no
great sacrifice to himself, and had attached
the condition that it should establish an
institution forever bearing his name.   Others
may add their gifts to that foundation until
it has grown far beyond the utmost hopes
of its founder, yet still must unnumbered
generations of musically voiced young women,
year after year, spell and chant in unison
that most unmusical name.   Does he deserve
it?   Surely no mortal man can claim so much!

You will cite John Harvard and Elihu
Yale, Ezra Cornell, Matthew Vassar, and
many others, but really they have no bearing
upon this question.   The collection of books
or the petty sums of money bequeathed by
John and Elihu are nothing in comparison
to the ideas which they modestly bequeathed,
the stimulus and the inspiration; and they
made no provision as to their names.   Cornell, Vassar, Durant, and others who founded

institutions while they were yet living gave not only funds, but years of anxiety, labor, and struggle, and at death left practically all of their fortunes, so that in each case the man and the institution were inseparable in the public mind, and the name was in most cases inevitable.

How much commemoration can a man buy with money? The purchasing value of a dollar changes so! If Robert K. Jones gave ten thousand dollars toward the endowment of a school for young women, and ten thousand dollars were of no great value to him, for how many centuries to come must visitors to the seminary listen to the chanted spelling of his unlovely name?

I understand that there are learned judges whose business it is to interpret clauses in bequests when they are of doubtful meaning and also certain state officers whose functions have to do with last wills and testaments. If I were some one of these functionaries I should long for the power to set precedents at once for the protection of all future beneficiaries against the clammy fingers of the dead hand. Robert K. Jones is entitled, let us assume, to just ten thousand dollars' worth of musical spellings of his name, and as the young women who chant it in unison become more numerous and more charming the purchasing value of the dollar grows less. I have no sympathy for him, and I would not allow him any bonus. He got his money's worth years and years ago.

The fact of the matter is that money is not worth so much as some philanthropists think it is. The well established superstition that anything a man gives as a benevolence must be accepted with thanks is in part responsible for this, and for the grip of the dead hand.

There is no closet so crowded with skeletons as is the Sunday-school library of sacred memory. Do you remember the books you drew from it in your youth? I think that the most perniciously harmful reading of my own early days was due to the ministrations of the Sunday-school librarian. The morbidly moral, the mawkishly sentimental, scratched deeper grooves on the surface of my young mind than all of the pages of *The Golden Days* or *The Fireside Companion* or the Nick Carter Library which I read surreptitiously in Tommy's woodshed. On those sanctified shelves were tomes deader than anything else under heaven that ever died—

for what is more thoroughly dead than discarded science and exploded theology, or even the sentimentality of an older generation? Every shelf in that library was clutched by the dead hand of some forgotten donor, because the librarian had not the courage to refuse, or the hardihood to burn the gift after its receipt. But, after all, who has? I remember hearing Miss Ida Tarbell say that she passed a most important milestone in her development when she gained the courage to burn a book. Our attitude toward printed books bound in covers was at one time akin to fetish-worship. Perhaps there is a by-product of good result in the present-day overproduction of books, in that we do not believe in type so implicitly as once we did. Perhaps people are at last learning to burn books which are not worth keeping, instead of giving them away to Sunday-school libraries and to the Salvation Army, and so acquiring merit for what is actually an evil deed.

A giver of gifts, if Scripture is to be believed, has his reward in the giving. If he gives worthless books that cumber up a bookshelf and, furthermore, requires of future generations that those books shall be pre-

served, his name should not be honored—
it should be anathema.   If he gives a library,
and specifies that his name shall be graven
forever above its portals, and then requires
of future generations that they shall maintain
the library and his name at their expense, it
is proper to ask whether he is not buying his
monument too cheaply. And if his dead
hand keeps a benumbing grip upon some
worthy activity of living souls, I am for laws
that will make it possible to relax that grip
and enable judges to call out in tones that
may be heard across the Styx, "The time is
up. You have got all the commemoration
you paid for."

A CHAIR OF NONSENSE

It is easy to talk sense! As babies we link up words into sentences that express reasonable ideas. It is true that the human animal in his primitive days, before he has come into his lingual heritage, often babbles in words of his own creation; or for a year or two shapes old words into strange uninherited phrases. "My dear, the child is talking nonsense!" Sometimes he croons his nonsense to tunes—nonsense tunes—of his own making. But all this is an art that he soon forgets and too often never regains.

Yes, it is easy for grown-ups to talk sense; quite as easy as for you now to retort, "Well then, why don't you do it?" Man's more obvious thoughts have all been formulated so many times that they have taken unto themselves fixed forms of expression which our tongues can instantly utter in response to the slightest impulse. "How do you do?" "Many happy returns of the day," "Trust

in an overruling Providence," "Truth is
stranger than fiction," "It's all for the best."
These are easy to say and easy to listen to,
because the tasks of formulation and inter-
pretation were performed long ago by those
pioneers who did our thinking for us.

So dominated are we by a reasonable world
that it is not only easy to talk sense, but hard
to talk nonsense. Try to talk pure nonsense
and willy-nilly (a great-great-great-grand-
father of a phrase is Willy-Nilly) you find
yourself conveying a meaning! The very
effort to avoid the conventional symbols of
thought is forcing upon you a most unusual
form of mental activity.

Whether axioms and maxims and other
crystallized forms of common sense be a
symptom or a disease, inevitably they increase as the race grows older and lazier, and
everything gets to be said. It is high time
that we should attack them by a powerful
antidote. With this aim in mind I propose
the establishment of Chairs of Nonsense in
our colleges and universities—those inner-
most sanctuaries of the Accepted Truth and
the Undisputed Thing. And I stipulate that
there should be courses offered to teachers
as well as to students.

The ideal university, we are told, is Mark Hopkins at one end of a log and a boy at the other—wisdom on one side of the desk, inquiry and challenge on the other. If wisdom becomes arbitrary, challenge becomes impertinent and useless. If challenge ceases, wisdom deteriorates into dull formula. But a little Nonsense on that log, and what a difference!

"We know what Lewis Carroll was in daily life," writes Gilbert Chesterton: "he was a singularly serious and conventional don, universally respected, but very much of a pedant and something of a Philistine. Thus his strange double life in earth and in dreamland emphasizes the idea that lies at the back of nonsense—the idea of *escape*, of escape into a world where things are not fixed horribly in an eternal appropriateness, where apples grow on pear-trees, and any odd man you meet may have three legs. Lewis Carroll, living one life in which he would have thundered morally against anyone who walked on the wrong plot of grass, and another life in which he would cheerfully call the sun green and the moon blue, was, by his very divided nature, his one foot on both worlds, a perfect type of the position of modern nonsense. His Wonderland is a country populated by insane mathematicians. We feel the whole is an escape into a world of masquerade; we feel that if we could pierce their disguises, we might discover that Humpty Dumpty and the March Hare were Professors and Doctors of Divinity enjoying a mental holiday."

Escape!—the word is crowded with joyous suggestion—escape and revolt. Listen to Algernon Charles Swinburne escaping from the slavery of dull poetic sense:

"From the depth of the dreamy decline of the dawn through a notable nimbus of nebulous moonshine,

Pallid and pink as the palm of the flag-flower that flickers with fear of the flies as they float,

Are they looks of our lovers that lustrously lean from a marvel of mystic miraculous moon shine,

These that we feel in the blood of our blushes that thicken and threaten with sobs from the throat?"

And hear Bishop Corbet escaping from theology in the seventeenth century:

"Like to the fiery tombstone of a cabbage,
Or like a crab-louse with its bag and baggage,
Or like the four-square circle of a ring,
Or like to hey ding, ding-a, ding-a, ding;
E'en such is he who spake, and yet, no doubt,
Spake to small purpose, when his tongue was out."

"He must be a fool indeed who cannot at times play the fool; and he who does not enjoy nonsense must be lacking in sense," wrote Rolfe, the great Shakespearean scholar. "None but a man of extraordinary talent," said DeQuincy, "can write first-rate nonsense." It is easy to prove that great men of all times have found in nonsense a refreshment of mind or a challenging test of mental vitality. Wisdom, grown wiser than its own formulas, turns from introspection in healthful outbursts of self-contempt. Nonsense is in fact perpetually challenging Sense. "It's better not to know so much than to know so many things that ain't so," says Josh Billings defiantly. "Truth is stranger than fiction," says Old Saw. "It is, to most people," says Mark Twain.

"I never nursed a dear gazelle,"
    softly quotes Tom Hood,
"To glad me with its dappled hide,
    But when it came to know me well,
    It fell upon the buttered side."

"*Think!*" cries Nonsense. "Your common
sense is clogging the machinery of ratiocination; your axioms soft-pedal the vibrating
strings of the mind." Thoughts are not
stimulated by any final statement of concrete
fact; they are set at rest. But a statement
which apparently means nothing at all will
at once set them going.

In attempting to justify my chair of Nonsense I am not content to quote DeQuincy
or Samuel Johnson or Lord Tennyson in
praise of it, or to cite the fact that Ruskin
placed Edward Lear at the head of his list of
one hundred best books. But we must
scrutinize the subject-matter itself and find
in nonsense intrinsic values sufficient to en-
title it to a place beside the Dead Languages,
Higher Mathematics, Household Economics,
Paleontology, and others of that sacred
company.

First of all, Nonsense bears some peculiar
and mysterious relationship to Truth. Per-

haps it is fourth dimensional truth. Perhaps it is the truth of to-morrow; undoubtedly, if Professor Einstein's theories hold good, many of the truths of to-day are nonsense. Perhaps it is truth upside down, and classes must stand on their heads to study it. Greater sacrifices have been made in the pursuit of wisdom.

But my theory is that Nonsense embraces All-Truth, even as infinitude embraces the universe. All of the sermons worth preaching could find their texts in Mother Goose, or in Lear, or in those other Bibles, the Alice books. Mr. Don Marquis, in a recent essay extolling the virtues of nursery rhymes, says that he himself forever thinks of royalty in terms of the King who was in his counting house and the Queen who ate bread and honey. And I daresay that the Old Lady Who Lived in a Shoe has wielded upon rising generations an indirect influence compared to which Froebel is negligible. Students might well devote much time to the study of Madam Goose to discover what it is that makes her sayings applicable to all sorts and conditions, generation after generation. Is it merely her simplicity of utterance—a lost art with so many of us—that gives her a cryptic and subtle sound? Edward Lear testified that he had a most difficult time, after he wrote his Nonsense Books, trying to prove that they were not political pamphlets, or at least satires upon current life and manners. Hundreds of readers were certain that they knew personally the "Dong with the Luminous Nose."

It occurs to me that nonsense does not mean anything in particular because it means everything. If this is the case, what other field offers so great opportunities for endless research? "What is it that I mean?" wrote Charles Battell Loomis:

"What is it that I mean,
  Oh, potent soul of mine?
  Oh, ecstasy divine
  In luscious meadows green!

"When from the void of things
  (What is it that I mean?)
  I sense the joys unseen
  And memory backward flings;

"When I encounter doubt
  And flee th' unquiet scene—
  (What is it that I mean?)
  Friend, hast thou found me out?

"A charnel house at e'en,
A dusky, reddened sky,
A tomb where none is nigh—
(What IS it that I mean?")

This questioning spirit is the basis of all
true education. But it must be questioning in
perfect honesty of heart; and where is there less
evasion and equivocation than in nonsense?

"Not understood? Take me hence! Take
me yonder!
Take me away to the land of my rest—
There where the Ganges and other gees
wander,
And uncles and antelopes act for the best,
And all things are mixed and run into each
other
In a violet twilight of virtues and sins,
With the church-spires below you and no
one to show you
Where the curate leaves off and the pew-
rent begins!"

So writes Barry Pain, and W. S. Gilbert
echoes, in a burst of perfect frankness:

"His gentle spirit rolls
In the melody of souls,
Which is pretty but I don't know what it
means."

Neither do I know what it means, but surely that does not prove it valueless; for I recall that in my own college days, as I painfully struggled through the pages of the "Anabasis," I was assured that I should value the experience in after life not for the information which Xenophon had written down, but for the mental training which I had gained in trying to find out what he meant. Why then, in all of these impressive curricula—set forth in many pages of college catalogues—is there no course deliberately entitled, "Nonsense, Its Literature, Its Uses, and Its Philosophy?" True, now and again some such course exists fortuitously, but its conductor is probably a prophet unawares.

May I be permitted finally to base my appeal for my Chair of Nonsense upon the established arguments of the upholders of higher education as it is? If the Curriculum Committee will but know that nonsense is the chaos out of which all truth was created they will at once grant that an intensive study of its elements may be a means finally of discovering the very secret of life; at any rate let them think of the mental training acquired by the student in trying to find out.

That a straight line, for instance, is the

shortest distance between two points is a
statement containing one truth, and one
only. What a regrettable paucity of con-
tent! Think of those beautiful lines of the
Icelandic poet as set down by George Ade:
  "To hold is not to have—
  Under the seared firmament
  Where Chaos sweeps, and vast Futurity
  Sneers at these puny Aspirations—
  There is the full Reprisal."
In this statement there may be a thousand
truths, for all I know. The fact that I cannot
point out any of them at the present moment
of writing is not in the least significant. But
I am somehow reminded of my own early
metrical interpretations of the ancient poets.
Doubtless any one skilled in the examination
of undergraduate literal translations could
gain something from it at a single glance.

Certain apologists for our higher education measure everything in terms of service.
All studies are of value in so far as they teach
man to know his fellow man. Then let Nonsense establish herself triumphantly. I may
utter sense to a passing stranger and we pass
on as strangers—but let me recite nonsense
to him, and at once our relationship becomes
positive. A common knowledge of current

literature makes conversation at afternoon
teas. An equal acquaintance with Egyptian
scarabs makes for envy, hatred and all malice.
But the discovery of a common familiarity
with "Sylvia and Bruno" and "Gentle Alice
Brown" will cause two hearts to beat as one.
"Don't tell me," said William Pitt, "of a
man's being able to talk sense. Everyone
can talk sense. Can he talk nonsense?"

I have discovered that if Jones's conversation consists of nothing but a succession of
exact truths, I do not necessarily get to know
Jones. I merely get to know the truths. But
if Jones says something which means nothing
at all, I feel that I must know him better. If
Robinson tells me all his exact symptoms
since he was sick, I know the symptoms,
and do not need to know the man. If he offers
to tell me how he was since before he was sick,
I study him with an aroused curiosity.

We devote the best years of our youth to
an examination of the wisdom of the dead,
in order that we may better know the living.
Why should we not, then, more systemati-
cally immerse the minds of our young in a
wholly confusing penumbra of ideas, and let
them work their way out by natural processes
of mental creation into All-Knowledge?

PEDAGOGUES AND BUSINESS MEN

THERE are plenty of people in the world who measure all values in terms of dollars and cents. "Body, mind, and soul, a man must in the long run be worth just about what he gets." Lately the fact has been widely advertised that teachers are not highly paid, and business men have been asked to surrender some of their surplus to aid the pedagogue. In every part of the country the response has been generous and prompt, but too often the appeal has been made as for a worthy charity. Teachers may not be worth more than they get, but for pity's sake, do not let them suffer! A business man who lives and breathes by economic law may still shrink from the thought of human suffering, and this argument is the direct route to his pocketbook. Urge merely the fact that teachers are underpaid, and he might at once retort that those who really are paid less than they are worth will take their labor to other markets.

A teacher who loves his work need not feel greatly concerned by such an appraisal of his value. But when he finds himself rated at even lower figures by one of his own order, then it is high time to take an account of stock. Some time ago, I read in a current magazine the frank confession of one who had been a college professor, entitled "Why I Remain in Industry." I can readily see, as I attempt to reply, that his cloak of anonymity must have spared him much embarrassment! I must try in a more impersonal fashion to set forth in the face of his various arguments why it is conceivable that a man might not return to industry who had gone from it into the vocation of teaching. My pen sticks a little at the use of the term "industry" as distinguishing commercial life from work in a college classroom. Some college professors are industrious, and some business men are not. But after all, any terms will do, so long as we understand each other.

It is hard to condense the arguments of seven magazine pages into a few paragraphs and present them fairly. However, my intentions are honorable. Deponent stated

that he left his faculty position "on leave,"
as did many others at the time, to go into
war work. As a scientist, he readily found
a place in industry as an expert. At the end
of the war he faced the alternative of re-
turning to college work or staying where he
was. Then follow his arguments in favor
of industry. The first is the question of
dollars and cents. He discovers that he
can earn more money in industry, and that
his salary will be increased at intervals to
keep pace with his increasing ability. He
contrasts the college situation, where he will
be paid inadequately, with promotion dependent not upon his increased usefulness, but
upon many other considerations of academic
expediency, such as the number of men of
his rank who watch him jealously; and the
number above him who are slow to die or
resign.

He notes that in industry, if promotion may
be blocked in his particular concern, his
"constant dealings with other industries put
him in the way of openings elsewhere";
whereas the university world disapproved of
any sort of effort at self-advancement. He
cannot write to other universities asking
them to consider him as an applicant; he is

told that such a thing simply "isn't done."
He must wait until he is invited. So he may
be pocketed in his own college, and forbidden
by custom to make any direct efforts whatsoever to get out, unless he leaves the profession altogether.

He dwells upon the fact that men of his age
of recognized inferior abilities, who at the
start chose to enter industry, now own comfortable houses, live in pleasant suburbs, ride
in their own cars, belong to country clubs, and
have time for tennis and golf. He does not
hanker for luxuries, but he looks upon these
things as common necessities, and as the
marks of a successful man, and he resents his
lack of them.

He says that as an instructor he had been a
man among children, dictating year in and
year out to immature youths, unable or unwilling to talk back, and he yearns to be "a
man among men."

He dwells on the common supposition that
business life is one of grind and anxiety and
rush for wealth, characterized by cold-blooded
inhumanity, and on the other hand that the
university is the reputed home of ideals.
He has lost this notion. He has found among
his business associates "a more active and

widespread interest in human affairs than during his entire academic career." Rather than theoretical, this interest was immediate and practical. The business man of to-day, not the professor, is the true idealist! College professors withdraw themselves from life, with an intellectual rather than an actual interest in the masses. They "would uplift humanity, but without stooping themselves in the process."

Then he dwells upon the vast material growth of the universities, millions and millions spent in palatial dormitories, ornate laboratories, magnificent stadiums, with only a pittance of these bequests set aside for the betterment of the human equipment. "Indeed," he says, "the proportion of money spent on material equipment and human equipment by most great universities offers a contrast in the light of which industry appears as an institution of charity." He then refers with evident earnestness to the comfort of having a secretary or stenographer and the other conveniences of business life which have made business experience peculiarly pleasant.

So far, he says, the advantages of an industrial career outweigh those of the academic; but the final argument upon which he places greatest emphasis is intellectual freedom. He claims a peculiar devotion to freedom of speech and action, and is stifled in an atmosphere of intellectual censorship, and here he asserts that the world of business most pleasantly contrasts with the college campus. He cites many instances to prove that our universities restrict freedom of thought.

His own summary I must put in his own words, though it most inadequately sums up his case: "To be in a position that calls forth all my creative powers; that brings me into contact with other generous and broad-minded men; that holds forth bright promise for the future; that pays me a salary sufficient to support my family in comfort; and above all, to be called 'Doc,' and regarded as an equal among equals—these are the conditions which finally decided me to give up my university career and remain in industry."

I think that we need not argue at any length the question of financial return. If college professors are still underpaid, it is done by institutions which now receive as students the sons and daughters of our wealthiest business men. A captain of industry who pays two thousand dollars a year to a preparatory school that makes his son ready for college, accepts college education for his son at a rate of four hundred dollars a year knowing that he is getting something for nothing, and suspecting that his son's teachers are underpaid. Business men serve as trustees of these institutions, and it is because of their final decisions that income has gone into equipment of buildings rather than into better payment for the teaching force. Or, if their hands are tied by the terms of bequests, it is because those terms were laid down by business men who preferred to leave buildings and material equipment as tombstones graven with their names, than to endow faculties. But they are dead, and doubtless are now surveying these questions with an omniscience I am unable to apply.

No, I shall not quarrel with my anonymous friend on the subject of salaries. Egotistically the teacher believes that in dollars and cents he is relatively far underpaid. He hopes that the men in industry who have made themselves responsible for the situation will see that future generations are more adequately rewarded, and he trusts that the funds will be raised without the use of such slogans and phrases as are current in drives for charity!

I would not give so much space to the financial side of the question if my ex-professor had not done so, and if the question had not been so widely discussed of late. Making money is a business in itself. Men can do that who can do little else. The teacher is engaged in other tasks that he finds of greater interest, the value of which can not be measured in dollars. He hopes that they will yield in time an adequate financial return, and for the sake of his family he must try to make them do so. In the meantime if he is paid less than it costs him to live and save, he has the satisfaction of knowing that he is extending charitable aid to a worthy college which for the time being is economically unsound.

Other arguments in this discussion deserve far greater consideration. Likelihood of promotion, for instance; ready recognition of talents and industry; fluidity of employment; these are matters of great importance, unless ambition is to be crushed and apathy take its place, and friendly emulation give way to jealousies and distrust. In the first place, we must be careful not to confuse instances with generalizations. My ex-teacher left one university to go into one business concern. I can cite business offices where jealousy is far more generally rife than in any college, where the very highest executive officer of them all regards with evident suspicion the rise of any one to a place near his level; and I have seen that spirit carry itself down through every grade. I have heard business men say that one of the most important future efforts in their establishments must be directed toward the development of *esprit de corps*, because their output is curtailed by the existence of ill feeling and distrust.

As for fluidity of employment in business and in teaching—the general manager of a railroad said some time ago: "I feel that I deal with two types of fellow manager, when I am looking about for men. If, for instance, I turn to Jones's road for a competent assistant, and offer one of his men higher place with me and better pay, Jones is angry. He seems to consider the matter a personal attack, and he makes both of us as sorry as possible that the offer was ever made. On the other hand, Brown considers it a compliment to his organization and his training if I offer one of his men higher place in my company. If he wants to keep the man, he makes a counter-proposition.   If he cannot afford to do that, he says to him, 'Accept the offer with my blessing; I can move Robinson up into your place.   At least it gives me a chance to reward a good fellow below you.' "

The ex-professor who rejoices that he is out of teaching and in business is fortunate in the concern which now employs him.   He might have been unfortunate.   He is right about the slowness of academic promotion, and this again is the old argument of dollars and cents; the rewards of teaching are not measured entirely by the speed of promotion.   But is not industry crowded with men of middle age living close to their incomes, and worried as to the future, afraid to bring up the question of a needed "raise" lest it might be a step in the direction of discharge?   In the university there is at least some sort of tenure of office law, and some protection against whimsical discharge.

As for the teacher's opportunities of higher place elsewhere, when promotion within his own university is blocked—the field is large, and the profession of teaching undermanned. College executives differ, just as railroad executives differ.   If an instructor desired to stimulate invitations from other institutions, for justifiable reasons of his own, why should he not go to his executive superior, make his reasons clear, and ask friendly assistance rendered in such a way that it would be an endorsement rather than a detriment? As for writing letters in his own behalf to persons who might be of aid, of course the question largely depends upon how such a letter is written. An officer in a business house hesitates to write to other business houses direct, offering his services, while he is still presumably in good standing in his own concern. "It isn't done," says the ex-professor. Of course it is done, just as much in the academic world as in the business world. If it is done right, it may be effective, and if it is done wrong, it injures the writer's chances, and quite properly so. We are both basing our arguments upon individual knowledge or experience. He says that he wanted to do it, and was told that he mustn't. I say that if a teacher wants to do it, he certainly should. It is one professor against another. Sic 'em, Tige!

It is the charge that teaching injures a man's personality which one finds most irritating. "As an instructor I was a man among children," confesses my anonymous writer, "dictating year in and year out to immature youths unable or unwilling to talk back," and he longs to be a man among men. Then for Heaven's sake why was he not a man among men? There are men enough; the fault lay with himself alone. Colleges unfortunately do know the type of teacher who is never a man among men, and that university is most blessed which has fewest of them. A teacher who "dictates" to immature youths usually influences them about as much as would a katydid. He misunderstands his function, which is not to provide them with ready-made conclusions. He it is who acquires the "professorial manner"— an unconscious affectation of omniscience. There are two or three men living who were my teachers in my undergraduate days, whose friendship I cherish to-day. As teachers they stimulated discussion. As I remember it, their students were neither unable nor unwilling to "talk back," but did a great deal of it. Those old teachers have spent a lifetime in the companionship of immature youths without losing manly force or the ability to be "men among men." Yes, both kinds of college professor exist, but surely the discouraged or debilitated one will do less harm in industry.

Does it not amount to this: that some men fail in the vocation of teaching just as some men fail in the world of business—because they are unfit for it? The qualities which unfit a man for one do not necessarily fit him for the other; neither realm wants the other's discards! But that a man should fail to find in his first choice those satisfactions which he discovers in his second proves nothing, except that he alone made a mistake which he was fortunate enough to correct in time.

The most interesting of the contentions in favor of industry contrast the practical idealism of business, and the visionary, vague, or ineffective idealism of the college. Two thoughts come to me in this connection. Industry is more and more demanding a college training for its directors. The new leaders of industry to-day are college-trained men. If they are bringing to business a practical idealism that is so warmly described, it is fair to assume—and in fact they frequently assert—that they gained it in their college years, under men who succeeded somehow in instilling it. If it is true that those instructors were unpractical, perhaps it was because their task had to do with theory—in the firm establishment of *principles* in the minds of embryo industrialists. Yet the ex-teacher I have been quoting is himself an example of the college professor who, when the nation's call came, left the classroom, and was able at once to make his training of service. He was willing to lay aside his robes and soil his shirt-sleeves in an industrial laboratory. It is a matter of worthy record that hundreds and hundreds like him did the same thing, and then, when the task was done, returned to the classroom to take up again the work that they liked best.

The final argument I have cited is that of intellectual freedom. It is true enough that there have been notable examples, even recently, of great universities which attempted to restrain their teachers in the expression of their views. Instances have received wide publicity, and it has been good for the health of higher education. But two or three facts deserve emphasis here, even in connection with these instances. Pressure was brought to bear not on what teachers thought or said but upon what they arbitrarily taught; and the pressure was exerted not by fellow teachers, but by certain business interests represented in the control of the college. Men of extreme conservatism, to say the best for them, acting in all sincerity and in the belief that they had a great responsibility to prevent the inroads of "pernicious" and "false" doctrine, took such action as they did. Are there no business firms which would in one fashion or another rid themselves of "radical" managers or foremen, especially if such men felt it their duty to be propagandists? I do not seek to justify—but merely to deny industry's superiority in this regard. It seems to me that a teacher should recognize two kinds of freedom, demanding the one and not the other. One is the freedom of belief, and the right to *express*, not to enforce, his conclusions. The other is the freedom to make an offensive noise just because it will be offensive to those with whom he differs. Of course it is foolish for a university to martyrize one of the noisy sort. There is a phrase recorded in New England colonial history which comes to my mind. It seems that the Quakers, who were the boisterous protestants of Roger Williams' day, were not a problem in his colony, nor had they been in Plymouth; for the simple reason that

neither colony barred them out. "For,"
said Roger, "they go only where they will
find trouble."

It is interesting to note the conflicting
testimony on this very subject. Our radicals
tell us that the colleges are refrigerators of
conservatism, where every teacher is an intellectual slave to the great financial interests
which have endowed the institution; or if it
be a state university, to the financial interests
which control the political party which elects
the legislature which votes the budget. On
the other hand, your conservative business
man is protesting that the colleges are hot-
beds of radicalism, that the best of them are
getting to be "Rand schools," and that every
crazy "ism" under heaven is represented on
our college faculties; and that if a radical
demagogue arises in the land, he is sure to
number among his followers a large group of
college professors. There is some comfort
to be gained from this conflict of testimony.

If our colleges were hermetically sealed, I
should think it possible that faculty and
students might pursue a serene course along
a road hewn and walled in by some long dead
intellectual pioneers of the institution. But
they are not so sealed, and neither the trus-

tees nor the men of their faculties have the power to make these open-eyed, newspaper-reading boys and girls think what they are told to think, and reach ready-made conclusions, unaware of conflicts raging in the world outside. The best that can be done is to help them to straight methods of thinking, to question intelligently, to recognize sincerity and distrust plausibility.

Enough of such contentious arguments! I have touched upon them one by one, well or ill, according to my lights, and yet I find myself conscious of the fact that there has been no direct answer to the question suggested by that unnamed writer, "Why should a college professor not go at once into industry if offered the opportunity, and consider himself flattered to boot?" It is not easy for one who dreads sentimentality to frame a complete answer. Let me touch on the lower motives first.

In the two-semester organization of the college year, still generally followed, there are only thirty-two weeks of actual teaching time. There are many ways in which the college professor may use the free third of his year. He is under obligation to keep himself in training professionally. He must acquaint himself by study with the new developments in his field. The same is true of the business man, but the latter must fight for time to give to absorbing study. Here, too, is time for writing, if the teacher possesses the inclination. And for three months at any rate there is time for the intelligent rebuilding of physical and mental vigor. It takes much in the realm of business to counterbalance that, even though professorial salaries are so low that it cannot be utilized to the fullest advantage.

Social developments to-day have brought about an increasing demand upon the college specialist as a lecturer, if he will but take the trouble to organize his material in a fashion to interest the layman. Such lectures are not only a source of added income, but they benefit the lecturer's own attitude. They have all the value of the business man's inventory of stock. The college teacher's social environment, instead of being narrow, is far more than horizon-wide. He finds that those engaged in the same occupation a thousand miles away are his neighbors, and those fellows in his own field are his friends. The name and repute of his university are his letter of recommendation to any circle.

There are, of course, disadvantages to the intimate community life of the campus. A university faculty has the combined faults of a small village and a wide family connection. There is a tendency to gossip, and it may be easy to begin a quarrel; but the gossip of a campus community does not compare in ill-nature to the gossip of a small suburb, and the petty squabbles are like those of a family connection. They are within the family, and if the attack comes from without, it is likely to bring about a united front.

The ex-professor whose article I have quoted found his happiness in industry, and all of those comforts which he feels are not really luxuries, but his by right. The man who continues in college teaching may find an immediate social environment equally satisfying: associates devoted to intellectual pursuits, who make very pleasant companions in such time as they can give to each other; living so much on the same scale, with such an amusing insight into one another's financial affairs that there is no struggle about appearances. His children are at least as well off as they would be in the average suburb, and better off than if he were in a city flat, taking the subway twice a day to his office. The average business man whose home is in pleasant surroundings leaves it at eight in the morning, and gets back to it after six at night. The hardest working college professor does better than that. The most famous artists and musicians come to his very doors, while lectures on all possible subjects are thrust at him until he hardly dares look the college calendar in the face. Yet he does not have to go. I think that on the social side an unprejudiced judge would say that the average college professor is more happily situated than the average business man.

But a reasonable contentment with environment is not the real answer to my question. I honestly believe that the great majority of teachers, and I have seen them in colleges east and west, stick to their profession because they feel that there they are on the firing line. That very conflict of evidence as to intellectual freedom which I have just cited shows that these colleges and universities are in the forefront of the battle over the really big issues of to-day.

It has been my lot to attend college reunions of many sorts. They are interesting phenomena, these assemblages of busy men who meet together to sing the praises of some alma mater, and to listen to over-long talks on idealism and lofty abstractions which surprisingly hold their attention. "Loyalty to one's Alma Mater" is a phrase used glibly among business men, and five times out of ten it represents a shallow thing, yet it must represent something. I have found myself sometimes trying to figure out just what it does mean, when used, for instance, by the somewhat unemotional and cold-blooded money-maker, who only that afternoon was working out business problems in an atmosphere remote from any such thought. I think that even in the case of that extreme type I have a clue to the truth. He recognizes that he is making a very slight contribution to the better side of present-day life. He suspects that actual world-progress must be an intellectual and spiritual, and not a material thing. He buys a little ease of spirit by contributions to charities and worthy "drives" of various sorts, but gives them no thought beyond the question of how much money to give. The better side of him calls for a spiritual contribution somewhat greater than this. He wishes that he had a

part in the real battles of his age, and if he
has any stuff in him at all, he is not content
that it should be wholly a vicarious part.
In his relationship to his old college he finds
that he actually "belongs" to an organization
which has no sordid aim whatever, and is
contributing to the solution of many questions.
Sometimes, when his business permits, and
when he allows himself to dwell upon this line
of thought any length of time, he tries hard
to make his relationship stand for something.
He tries to get nearer to the firing line.   He
leaves his business for a day or two, goes to
his college, and attempts gropingly to take
part in the actual discussion of its problems,
and to help to shape its policies.   "Loyalty
to Alma Mater" is in reality a subconscious
belief in certain fine abstractions, as well as loyalty to the memory of his own youth.   Sometimes he finds that he can give his time in
greater measure, and he does so, with the
result that he is elected trustee of his own or
another college, and places his business abilities at the service of the institution.   He
has been appointed, from civilian life, to a
place of high command!   The average college-trained business man would sacrifice
very much to gain a college trusteeship.   Its

attainment is a proof that he serves in a greater cause than that of money changing; that he has been examined before a court higher than a court of trade and found to possess qualities worthy the honor.

A cynic may remark that appointment by this court is sometimes purchased by cold cash; but that is when there are business men of like calibre on the board. Such men sell degrees for dormitories! I do not mean to focus attention too much upon boards of trustees; but the college is under fire and they are its chief officials. They are drawn mainly from industry where my ex-professor claims to find the highest idealism. Yet they must be held responsible for some of these allegedly evil academic conditions. Every university has its devoted, self-sacrificing directors. Some may be handicapped by one or two of the other sort. Is there anything more unworthy a place in the university world than a trustee who has secured this honor and gives the college in return no skilled business service? He will not work and he does not resign. He is cheating society and cheating the college. His nearest competitor in unworthiness is the dispirited college professor who drudges dully through an endless grind. Yet the latter is less culpable. He has weakened under pressure.

But after all, am I not paying too much attention to the wrong kind of college officer? Such a type sticks out like a sore thumb, but like a sore thumb he is only one finger in ten.

Yes, the teacher likes to believe that he is on the foremost firing line. It is a service that demands not only training but an adaptability that training cannot give. "Things are in a bad way here," said a lawyer friend earnestly, as we stood together on a college campus. "These boys are talking about things they don't know anything about! Can't somebody stop them? They're playing with fire. I hear some of them actually call themselves Bolsheviki or something as bad!"

No, Counsellor, nobody can stop them. When you and I were in college some of these things were undreamed, and so we played with such fire as we had—Didn't you as a junior dare to call yourself an atheist?— and much of it wasn't even intellectual fire. Couldn't your teachers have taken it away from you, somehow?

"It's not the same thing. You're evidently getting tarred yourself. I wish I could talk to 'em."

Often and often have I heard him and his kind talk to them. With the benevolent manner of an old-fashioned Sunday school superintendent, he doles out ready-made idea-lets, and immature youth lolls in its seat listening appraisingly. Afterward all the judgment one can win from some young commentator who is as yet lamentably savage but confoundingly clear-eyed, is, "I've heard all that. Why did he leave out the real reasons, the poor fish?" C'est la guerre, Counsellor. You cannot fight with poor ammunition, or unprepared.

The deprecator of college teaching complains that the academic life holds too much aloof—that there is too great a line of demarcation between the world and the campus. I am inclined to make small defense of such a charge, and let the deponent continue to complain. It seems to me that definite advantage comes from a certain amount of academic detachment. The two realms should be coöperative and highly essential to one another, but there is no reason why one should swallow the other and assimilate it. I like to think of a realm of business which offers to the college its best representatives, to organize and direct the business side of the college community, and then denies to those representatives any right of idleness. I like to believe that in return Business receives from the college revitalizing young men with well organized thinking apparatuses, plus ideals. I like to think of academic life as so far cloistered that Truth may walk there on occasion, ungowned by expediency, and unashamed. Each realm should provide for the other the best experts that it can train, but just so soon as one attempts to *dictate* to the other how this training shall be organized and what shall be its final tests, then the harmonious coöperation is sure to cease, and the whole satisfactory relationship runs askew. There must above all be mutual respect, neither realm judging the other by the incompetents within its ranks.

"A few hours a week for a few years in the class room near a teacher, cannot compete with numberless long winter evenings near a home bookshelf."

—CHALDEAN PROVERB.

A BOOK IN THE HOUSE

GOOD books are living things. I know this is true because I have seen some grow. A few in particular come to mind because they and I grew up together. "Water Babies," for instance; that was a very young book when I was a little boy. It told a simple story in a childlike way. Then it kept getting more between its covers as we grew older. Now it has become a very wise book indeed. "At the Back of the North Wind" behaved in the same way. I suppose some cynic will claim that this wisdom was in the book all the time. But I know better. Indeed, there are many books that quite outgrow the men who wrote them and get to have much more in them than their authors ever put there. I think that this has happened to many of Shakespeare's plays and I am sure it is true of several books of the Bible.

To have spent a childhood without playfellows is a serious handicap for anyone to overcome; but it is not much worse than a childhood without several good books to grow up with.

I may not guess aright any of your boy friends, but if you numbered among them Tom Sawyer or Tom Canty, Jim Hawkins or David Balfour, or such older companions as John Ridd or Amyas Leigh, I'll wager they are almost as real to you now in recollection as the lad who lived in the next block. If they have grown along with you just as he did, then they have had quite as large a share in shaping your personality.

"Do you know Walt Whitman?" says somebody to me.

"Yes, indeed. Do you?"

"Pretty well; but I hope to know him better."

The good gray poet died before our day, yet here we are talking of him as a common acquaintance. We speak of *knowing* Dickens or Browning or Stevenson or the modern Russians, and we mean only that we have read them. Yet on second thought, I think we mean just what we say.

I knew O. Henry in the flesh. A dozen friendly letters from him are among my treasures. A silent man as to his own affairs;

quiet, unobtrusive. Could I say that I knew him if I had not read him? Do I know him much better, for that short period of acquaintance, than do the thousands of readers to whom he addressed his storied fancies? He has chatted gayly and gravely with them, heart to heart, offering far more of himself to them through their eyes than he offered to me through my ears. It is only because I am of their company also that I gain a mite of advantage.

"When I was a lad," said a passing acquaintance, "I saw much of Bret Harte; and I didn't think much of him."

"Ever read him?"

"No. Never wanted to."

Which of us knew Bret Harte—he, with the door of his understanding shut by prejudice, or I, who, never having seen him, yet seek the companionship of his many moods again and again, from the whimsy humor of his condensed novels to the dramatic pathos in some of his stories?

The point of all this palaver is a trite one, to be sure, but it needs resaying now and then. My little library is *peopled* by my books. Am I bringing together into the cozy space as broadening, as satisfying, as cosmopolitan a fellowship as I could wish?

It is as true as gospel that Mark Twain and Stevenson and Charles Lamb and Ben Jonson sought and still seek my friendship. Something of themselves, undoubtedly, they gave to corporeal friends and other relations in their years of early pilgrimage. But ninety-nine per cent of themselves, as they pored over their writing, they were forever offering in exchange for the friendship of readers-yet-to-be. It is for me to accept or reject.

I am one of those who believe that To-day is, on the whole, better than Yesterday, and that To-morrow may be better still; because To-morrow can, if it will, possess all the To-days and Yesterdays that ever were. Such optimism does not interfere with my regret over some of Yesterday's discarded treasures. People are so inclined to intemperance in their enjoyment of To-day. Motoring isn't better than walking; it is merely more than walking; the two are not to be compared. Yet there are those who have almost forgotten how to walk. I am comfortably certain that before long some indefatigable modern dancer in a moment of satiety will rediscover the

minuet or the De Coverley and love it. Then
he will be the enviable possessor of that and
the toddle or the woggle or the one-step as
well.

Moving pictures just at the present moment tend to crowd out books, particularly
with folk who have discovered the great
enjoyment that they gain from thus having
the surfaces of their minds tickled. It becomes increasingly troublesome for them to
enjoy anything which demands a greater
mental activity. Having learned to ride in a
motor car, they are likely to forget how to
walk.

The movies are undoubtedly a new art, or
let me say a new medium for artistic expression. Crude, inartistic, dull, even nasty-
minded experimenters have been messing
around in that medium and are still doing so.
But gradually one may see appearing out of
it all a number of hopeful efforts and some
great pieces of work. But moving pictures
do not exist instead of the spoken drama or
instead of books. They are merely one thing
more; and by reason of them our To-morrows
may be the richer.

But just at the present moment some
people have forgotten books, and a great

many young people are in danger of never discovering them. A book may be had for the price of a theatre ticket, but there are many who, if offered the choice, without the privilege of possessing both, would take the more perishable thing; for them a book is no more than a book. They do not know that acquaintance with a new book brings a new acquaintance permanently into their circle— that its friendship is a satisfying human friendship. Do you remember the two chorus girls who were discussing what they ought to give the leading lady for a Christmas present? One said, "Why not give her a book?" The other answered, "Gee! no; she's got a book."

My companionship with a book has this peculiarity—that there can be no back talk in any conversation between us. Yet there are times with all of us when we pause merely out of politeness to allow for responses. We don't want answers to our merely rhetorical questions, whomsoever we are with. We seek a chance to voice our own moods, and we cannot do it satisfyingly unless we have a sympathetic listener. Then again there are times when we are quite content to be silent while the companion we have sought does the talking. Books bring such companionship.

I know a group of lively, healthy-minded young people—in fact it is my business to know successive groups of them—who love pure nonsense for its own sake. Yet an astonishing number of them do not know *Lear*, or *Sylvia and Bruno*, or the *Bab Ballads*, or the *Ingoldsby Legends*, or even Oliver Herford and Guy Carryl and Gelett Burgess and Carolyn Wells and all that joyous company, living and dead. For these young folks of the new generation all, from Carroll to Carryl, are equally alive, and extending glad hands of welcome to the brotherhood. It is not that my young friends reject this advance; on the contrary, they do not know it has been made.

What books shall I invite to live with me? There are more in the world than I have means for or room for, whether mine be a six-foot shelf, or one with as many feet as a centipede; and there must be many that could never be my friends either because of their shortcomings or because of mine. Many folk I meet here and there that I am glad of meeting or the better for meeting—

and then I go home thanking God that I do not have to live with them.

The books that I want to have living in my house are those that I might enjoy rereading at one time or another. Not necessarily rereading all through, mind you. I want to know once and for all the whole of my friend's life, so far as he will bare it to me. Then it is our common property. But some of his views, his philosophies, and his experiences I will demand again and again even though I want only to quarrel with them. If a man says to you that he has no time for the re-reading of his books, regard him with suspicion. He will have no time to poke his head in at a friend's door and shout "Hello!" in passing.

Rereadings are intimacies that brook no full exposure. I imagine that a truthful account of them from the record of any man's winter evenings would be a surprising revelation of whimsicality even to himself. The other night, standing up in front of the book-case, I reread Lanier's "Marshes of Glynn," and then I sat down to D'Artagnan, where he regains his three friends in the three inns along the road to Amiens. And whatever else I reread is nobody's business but my own.

Rereading, I suspect, is a sort of vaga-bondage. There are other born tramps in this world besides those who walk abroad. Fifty per cent of me, I am sure, is innate vagabond and the other half enjoys safe anchorage. But the two are not so absolutely incompatible. Seeing the world is largely a matter of seeing its people. If the world will but pass by you, you can see the world though you stand still. But you must keep looking; and you must look behind faces and look twice at good pages, for in such a vaga-bondage the revisiting of favorite places in many books plays no inconsiderable part. If you do not do this, you see no more than the motor tourist who remembers Domrémy because he changed a tire there.

So, though I cannot steal rides to-day on through freights or beg passage on cattle steamers, because of certain pleasant chains, yet I am forever traveling. Motion is a relative thing. A whole audience in a cinema theater feels itself rushing along on a motor car because the fields and houses fly by in the other direction on a screen. I cannot keep a procession of friends and acquaintances from everywhere moving through my guest room—though we do our best. But new book acquaintances may tarry on the center table and a multitude of book friends snuggle into our shelves and constantly make me to feel that I am foot free in a stimulating world.

"Home training is like home cooking; it isn't infallible. It can't be much better than its ingredients."
—EPHRAIM STEBBINS.

A DOG IN THE HOUSE

WHEN does a house, slowly emerging from a chaos of lumber, bricks, and mortar, and taking on form and substance, cease to be merely a house and become a home? Surely before it is finished; no house which is the dwelling place of its owners is ever finished. Like the corporeal city of New York, each piece of furniture is on trial, each bit of carpet may be torn up to make way for a successor more in keeping with the owner's present state of prosperity. A woman is the centre of the home, to be sure. She is the true home-maker. But it is not Home solely because she is there. Several elements are needed which she welds into one unified whole. Strangely incongruous elements they may be— books; worn furniture, worn in such ways as to prove that it has contributed to comfort, and not merely to appearances; bits of handi-work here and there, embroidery or patches or what you will. Battered toys are a satisfactory element: I do not hold with those household efficiency experts who believe that a child's toy should never be discovered outside of the nursery. Children should be directed to keep their belongings within the nursery, to be sure, but the visitor gains at once a certain feeling of confidence in the homeliness of that home where he stumbles upon a wee fire engine across the doorway or sits upon a crippled doll in the parlor arm-chair.

Pets are an important element. How perfectly a weather-beaten rabbit or a tortoise trailing its broken tether work into the picture! Mr. Noyes has written a poem describing the way in which Nature, with her weather stains, paints the ugly newness out of man-made things. In the same way the director of the home manages somehow to take this broken toy, that old chair, a kitten or two, and all the flotsam and jetsam of living, and piece them together into a more wonderful mosaic than all the arts of our modern civilization have been able to fabricate with other materials.

He seemed all legs, like a cuttle-fish, as I carried him in my arms to the nearest street car.

"You can't bring a dog like that on here," said the conductor.

"But it's just a young little puppy," I protested. ·

"Little puppy your Grandmother!" said the conductor irrelevantly, and rang his bell.

He would neither walk forward independently, nor be led. Whichever direction I essayed, he braced his feet and slid. I felt that his head, which waggled loosely upon his shoulders, would inevitably pull off, and disclose a long pasteboard neck, after the style of those Easter rabbits that are filled with candy; so I lifted him in my arms again, there in the crowded city streets, intensely conscious of an aroused public amusement as I struggled to reenfold this or that hairy protruding tentacle.

Experience has taught me that there is no graceful method of carrying either a large puppy or a small boy struggling to be free. City blocks seemed to me that day to be miles in length and the baggage car of my suburban train was a haven of refuge, a flowery bed of ease. Yet always in my mind was the thought that there would be new struggles and humiliations at the final stage of my progress—from train to house. I found myself saying over and over, with all sorts of variations, "Water quench fire, fire burn stick, stick beat dog, for dog and I have *miles* and *miles* to go before we reach home!"

Up a certain new-made path I came, dragging my reluctant quadruped, his legs braced against me, his frowsy neck stretched to the danger point. On the porch, littered with the trash of building operations, stood the home-maker, waving a greeting. Behind her a temporary front door gaped hospitably open. An orchestra of saws and hammers played a rough welcoming chorus. Suddenly the taut chain in my hand grew slack. My sprawly captive wobbled past me, mounted the steps and sat down before the door, facing the path by which we had come. An unknown workman approached with a board upon his shoulder. Our drafted recruit arose to his full stilted height and barked his first warning of danger—barked with such tremulously eager violence that the effort tumbled him over; but behold, he had become a watch-pup, and this was Home!

In time the house stopped growing, at least in outward dimensions. Not so its guardian. He took on length and breadth, and visible cubits were added to his stature with every passing week. As he grew bigger he grew blacker, turning from a dusty nondescript rustiness to a glossy blackness from nose-tip to tail. The Hound of the Baskervilles was with us in the flesh, but not in the spirit. What his spirit was I find it hard to say. Put the soul of Puck into a clumsy container, modify it by an emotionally affectionate temperament, and you have something approximating the truth.

I have never been wholly patient with those who generalize disparagingly about certain breeds of dog. "Fox terriers," says a certain flat-dweller, "are irritable and snappy." "Collies," says another, "are dangerously temperamental."

Grant me a lively, impetuous disposition and then shut me in a superheated flat many hours of every day, and I will snap. Let me dress you in furs in warm weather and then urge you repeatedly to run and fetch a stick within a narrow yard—you will become dangerously temperamental. Some breeds of dog have certain natural environments. Out of those environments they are uncertain of themselves, often suspicious, and easily startled into regrettable action. Give a collie meadows to roam, sheep to herd, or, lacking sheep, a "gang" of wide-ranging small boys, and his own times for resting, and then you will have one of God's finest gifts to man, a trustworthy responsible dog. Give a fox-terrier earth for digging, small game or fellow pups for fighting, something to chew, something to chase, and he will be as faithful and alert a friend and servant as heart could wish.

Alas for the unhappy lot of many dogs! It is only the exceptional individual in any breed, more often among the bulls and terriers, that finds its natural environment in a city house and street; unless it be for those wee anomalies which Brother Irvin Cobb shockingly alludes to as "fur-bearing cock-roaches"; and perhaps also for their first cousins who lack the fur and are ever shivering in consequence. But are they indeed dogs?

As for the dane, because I love the tribe so well I shall speak with diffidence, hesitating at generalizations and holding close to one unmelancholy specimen, which, from puppyhood to elephantine adolescence, bumbled daily from bedroom to garden, from kitchen to attic, making the house and our hearts his own. Yet I am going to venture the following general assertions and then humbly await their destruction at the pen of some wiser caninologist. The dane is no more nearly related to a mastiff than he is to a St. Bernard. The greyhound is his nearest kin. Yet his blundering masters in past years, chiefly in this country, have bred him with thick legs and neck and heavy jowl. Having the heart of a greyhound in the body of a mastiff, he has been as uneasy of spirit as a collie in a city dwelling.

"It is faithful and trustworthy," says a certain encyclopædia, "and when first introduced into England was a favorite companion of both ladies and gentlemen; but when the order came into force commanding all dogs to be muzzled, this hound, having a will of its own, rebelled against being held in check, and being very strong, could not easily be kept under control, so had to be abandoned as a companion. It is now chiefly used as a show dog, but in the middle ages it was a sporting dog, and was employed to hunt the wild boar and chase the deer"—and so on, through many highly creditable paragraphs.

Let me hazard another generalization (observe how easily the didactic manner lays hold on one!). A dog possessing speed and strength relies naturally upon those traits in emergency.   The instinct of a hunting dane is to hurl its weight upon the foe.   Teeth as weapons are an afterthought.   A great dane that readily snaps or bites is a dog with misdirected energies.

As for our guardian, he steadily grew in size and glossy blackness, in whimsical mischief, in *personality* and in devotion.   The feeding was no serious matter.   He ate everything.   Two elements were to be considered in preparing the food—filling and nutrition; two parts filling to one part nutrition.   Table scraps of every sort, even to fruit peelings, were grist for his mill.   He was not an embarrassment in this regard—he was a useful institution.

An embarrassment he was in many ways. Demonstrations of affection from one hundred and twenty pounds of dog may be accepted in spirit, but in the flesh they were as the advances of an amiable earthquake.   There would come a troubled look in his soulful brown eyes when his struggles for some inadequate resting place upon his mistress's lap went unrewarded; and he would insinuate himself into incredibly small spaces to find room upon a sofa beside any one of us.

Rebuffs touched him so deeply that they,

too, were the cause of embarrassment. It
was his immediate wish when rebuked to
retire under something—the lower it was, the
better. When his spirits returned, as they
invariably did, and he arose to full height,
forgetting first to crawl out, he was likely to
leave the room with a small table or chair
perched jauntily upon his back. Nosing under
a rug was, on the other hand, a constant
delight, and I picture him standing gravely
before me with some gaudy Turkish garment
that he himself had donned covering him
from head to tail, his bright eyes gleaming
up at me from under one end of it while the
other end wagged heavily.

He had the ways of a terrier, and like a
handsome boy who has grown over-tall, he
seemed ever to be deploring his size. Perhaps the safest generalization about a proper
dane is to say that either he never realizes
he is not a lapdog, or always regrets that he
is not.

Some time ago an old friend whom I had
not seen for several years accosted me in the
street.

"Married?" he inquired, after other time-
bridging questions.

"Yes."

"Any children?"

"Three. And you?" I added.

"Boy and girl—four and six." Then he looked at me thoughtfully for a moment, seized my lapel and drew me outside the current of traffic. "You tell me *one* story about your kids," he burst out, "and I'll tell you one about mine!"

Dog owners are like parents in this respect —on their tongue-tips hang accounts of precocious acts, or deeds displaying almost human intelligence, and the careless acquaintance may unwittingly touch some hair-trigger that discharges the whole narration upon him.

Are you not, gentle dog-owning reader, pursuing these very pages with a certain friendly impatience, your thoughts flitting back and forth from your dog to mine? Are you not quivering to interrupt at my first pause for breath, with a "How interesting!— But I must tell you about our Fido—you've no idea how bright he is."

I will gladly listen to your panegyric, when you have heard mine.

I will even love your dog with you—if he be a *real* dog—on your say-so. Ah me, how easy it is to come to love a dog! And when there is so much dog to love, his hold upon one's affection becomes very great. "No man is so poor," says Josh Billings, "but what he can own a dog, and I have known some so poor they owned three." I am poor enough to have owned several sizes of dog; but without disparagement of any lesser breed within the law I exhort you at one time or another in your lives, for your soul's good, to get to know a dane. I would have you watch this giant body with its heart of a child gravely stalking some small beetle through the grass. I would have you note his lofty condescension toward inimical small dogs—his eager playfulness with friendly ones who always enter into games with him in a spirit of fearful bravado, wagging their tails violently throughout, as an earnest that no chance act of theirs should be misunderstood.

I would have you see him dig—not merely to hide a bone, but for the fun of digging. A wonder to the neighborhood was the hole our black genie dug beneath an ancient tree-stump. Straight into the ground he would crawl—under and between the roots completely out of sight; emerging finally on the other side like some buried mammoth exhuming itself.

I would have you swim with him, for his speed and power and reserve strength in the water are joys to behold. Often have I, and others with me, held to a powerful black tail and trailing out almost flat on the water been drawn many yards to shore.

Though a dane be first cousin to a greyhound, his tail is surely younger brother to that of a kangaroo. It steers him, it balances him like a gyroscope, and when he would bring his great weight to a sudden stop, it goes round and round in swift revolutions like a reversed propeller on an air ship. He is forever flailing it against some unfriendly corner and bruising the tip; then—yes, I admit it to his disadvantage—he goes about slapping little blood marks against walls and whimpering in grieved surprise at each new pain.

Obviously there are disadvantages to a dane. Humbug though he be ofttimes, since he has the dignity and bearing of a panther timid strangers refuse to consider him a humbug. Well intentioned though he is, yet those growls that seem to emanate from some sub-basement of his physical structure are enough indication for many sceptic friends, who prefer not to trust to his intentions. He is not a wise investment for gregarious folk in a crowded neighborhood. And yet in my effort toward a dispassionate consideration I have gone too far. There are many facts on the other side of the scale. He will not fight with neighbor's dogs—he is too big. Little aggressors he bowls over with a blow of his shoulder. As a draft animal for the children who come to know him he is invaluable, and for the littlest he is better than a dozen hobby horses.

Yes, thou unbeliever, I grant that this is a picture of one particular dane, drawn from loving memory. I will believe your stories of this or that dangerous monster of a beast. But I have heard, too, of treacherous collies and even mad poodles; and on the other hand I have learned that there are many other danes like mine; I have learned of them on those pleasant idle occasions when I have happened upon one dane-owner or another, and stepping out of the stream of traffic for a moment have listened to one story about his dog and told him one about mine.

Humbug was a term I used a moment ago, and though it may be written with a smile, yet there are good grounds for it now and then. Since knowing and coming to love the breed

I have entered a kennel of strange danes, whose basso profundo growls and gnashing teeth seemed to welcome me to instant destruction. I have not, I assure you, the disposition of a lion tamer. It was simply that each stately head and lithe body seemed to be but a replica of my own dog-chum, clad for the moment perhaps in some other colored garment. And as I pushed through the gate I found myself swayed this way and that by struggling monsters who wished to have their heads scratched. Listen to this corroborative testimony from a friend. She visited her Adirondack camp after a long absence. Dane pups had been born and had grown to dog's estate since she had last inspected the property. She missed her guide and caretaker at the station, and went alone to the camp, where no one was on hand to greet her. Letting herself in at the front door she was startled by a chorus of blood-curdling growls, and found herself facing three full-grown danes on guard.

"I had heard it said," she told us in recounting the affair, "that one's only safety when at the mercy of fierce animals lies in calm and ordinary behavior. With my heart beating violently, I looked for some commonplace

act to perform. Ashes had blown out from
the fireplace over the floor. A broom stood
handily by. The moment I reached for it
those formidable beasts leaped, as one dog,
out of the room. One of them went through
an unopened window, taking the sash with
him. It seems that the broom handle which
I had touched was the utensil used by my
guide for maintaining discipline among the
dogs."

We miss our black familiar—miss his in-
quiring whine at the door of a morning, his
companionship upon every sort of expedition,
his petty sins and his contrition, his hum-
bugry, his enormous weeping for infinitesimal
punishments. We miss him as a warm footstool beneath the table where he would lie
patiently throughout meal time, happy to
serve in that humble capacity. And if this
be his individual picture, painted with the
colors of prejudice, as a sort of memorial to a
dead friend, yet I dare assert that here and
there among my readers dane owners will
cry out, "He might have meant our Bis-
marck, our Prince, our Osra, when he wrote
that!"

FROM THE NOTEBOOK OF AN UN-NATURALIST

As for me, I want a pet that is at least conscious of error. The chief difference between man and the lower animals lies in man's capacity for sinning. Obviously he has no monopoly of the virtues. A dog may be faithful, an elephant may be kind and true, a cat is said to love home and fireside; the parental instincts of the penguin would put nine-tenths of the leaders of our best society to shame. It is not by possessing such attributes that animals become "almost human." It would be fairer to our furred and feathered friends to say that the man who possesses these traits in fine degree is almost animal. There is a horse of vaudeville fame that reckons simple sums in addition, and answers a wide variety of questions, if my memory serves me; I will even allow him to

194

write his own first name with his hoof in the sand. The show-bills call him "human," yet we feel no sense of kinship as we watch the performance, even though we should grant him all the powers his exhibitors claim. We simply say, "What a wonderfully clever horse!"—bestow a word of praise upon his trainer, and that is the whole story. I have seen a dog perform agile tricks with prompt obedience and obvious enjoyment, and to me he was still a dog. But when some canine friend hides on his wash-day; when he steals the cat's milk and pretends he did not; when he slinks in at a door with every expression of eye and limb crying "Peccavi," ah, then I say to myself, "There is something human about that dog."

In formulating this theory we must presume that a sin, to be a sin, creates a consciousness of violated moral law. A kitten after a canary or entangled in a skein of yarn retains an untroubled conscience—if you will grant a conscience to a cat even for purposes of argument. But a bronco which has devoted an hour to general devilment, putting her ears back and wearing an expression of confirmed viciousness, perhaps scraping her rider off against a tree, a little later will show contrition by her every act, and prove a definite consciousness of sins committed.

There are many dogs that have awakened in me this sense of human kinship, and some horses, and elephants that one has read about. Cats or parrots have never done it, nor rabbits nor white mice. I have seen such animals trained to exhibit cleverness, but I never yet saw one exhibiting remorse. Not only parrots, but birds in general I had always thought incapable of human foibles and failings. True, they are dainty and beautiful things, and one who does not enjoy them as neighbors, and desire to cherish and protect them, is not a very good citizen of this footstool. But a specific individual bird somehow never seemed to me to possess *personality*. Its mental or moral experiences seem quite remote from mine! This at least was my feeling (if I had bothered to analyze it) until a recent investigation into the alleged behavior of certain woodpeckers quite upset my attitude of mind.

In the state of Maine many things happen which are not down in the books, particularly the statute-books. Fish in Maine are of incredible weight, as proved by their own scales; the marksmanship of Maine hunters is akin to that of Natty Bumpo; and the prowess of all other woodsmen as *x* is to any mere known quantity. For these reasons I listened with placidity to the account of a coterie of depraved woodpeckers who were seen several times in advanced stages of intoxication. Yet in due time the circumstances of the story began to stir my curiosity.

Two large white birch trees, spared for the shade they gave, were standing quite alone in our camp's central clearing. A dozen or more log-cabins in a semicircle rimmed this campus, all facing those two trees out in the open and overlooking the pond whose shores roughly completed the circle. One of these trees was dead when we first saw it, and as full of holes as a sieve, up and down its trunk. A year later we revisited the camp, and behold, the other tree was evidently following its companion. " 'Twas woodpeckers did it," I was told. "They dug the first holes fer one reason or another. Then they come back later and found the sap that was standin' in them holes had got hard. It seemed to hit 'em in the right spot. The whole crowd got tight."

"What?"

"Lit up—spiflicated—dead drunk. We

could pick 'em off the tree with a noose at the end of a fishin'-rod."

"Poor things!"

"Poor things nawthin'! They kep' comin' back fer more, and dug new holes till they killed the tree."

It was this first statement of the case that I heard with placidity. One hears so many careless assertions from time to time about the use of intoxicants in Maine.

I referred to the yarn casually as I sat in one of the cabins that evening, partaking of crackers and ginger-ale.

"Well," said my host, "something made those birds sick."

"You saw them?"

"I held one in my hand."

It is annoying to feel oneself the butt of a concerted joke. Many tall stories from one friend are all in the day's play. One tall story from several friends argues oneself an object of ridicule. Absent-mindedly I accepted a proffered clove and departed, ruminating. There approached in the dusk an elderly serious-minded Boston business man, evidently seeking the oasis I had just left. I stopped him with the direct attack, "Did you ever see one of these woodpeckers around here drunk?"

"They aren't all woodpeckers; there are yellow-bellied sapsuckers among 'em," he evaded, and hurried on toward the beckoning lights.

The pursuit of trout for a day or two drove any thought of other researches from my unscientific mind. But a few mornings later, as we sat repairing our kits, a peculiar and resonant rattle broke the quiet of the place. "There goes Old Reliable ag'in," remarked the guide.

I followed his glance and saw a bird perched on the brass ball that topped the little flag-pole of our dining-cabin. He was busily tapping it with his beak. "Does he think there's a worm in that" I asked—"or juice or something?"

"Naw; he's been there before. He ain't a fool, by a long sight."

"Is he drunk?"

The guide regarded him solemnly. "No, he ain't drunk; he's just disturbin' us for the fun of it."

Not drunk, but disorderly! I got up and watched him as he flew away. There was a certain pertness in his manner of flying. Obviously this was one of that band of roystering camp-followers, and I followed him with my eyes till he was lost to sight in the woods. "There's something human about that bird," I found myself saying.

At a city dinner-table, after camping days were over, we mentioned our Maine woodpeckers and were laughed to scorn. As is often the case, the challenge of these skeptics made us advocates where before we had been neutral.

"No, we did not see them intoxicated. We saw those who had seen them. We saw the trees full of holes. We saw the birds. Some of them even woke us in the morning tapping on our cabin roofs and drain-pipes." But this was not enough. Shame upon us for presenting such weak evidence! Then and there I vowed to search for affidavits, experts, whatsoever those scoffers demanded to silence their scoffings. If I could not prove the case against my Maine woodpeckers, I would show up the depravity of the whole woodpecker tribe in general.

First of all I resorted to an old friend, an eminent editor claiming some acquaintance with birds and beasts.

"Your story is obviously improbable from the very start," said he. "A woodpecker does not drink sap, nor does he drill a hole in

a tree unless his instinct informs him that
there is a bug or worm inside. If that tree
was as full of holes as you say, it must have
been so full of bugs or worms that it was dead
before the woodpeckers attacked it. Therefore it could not have had any sap."

Meekly I called attention to the woodpecker who tried at regular intervals to make
a hole in the brass ball on top of a flag-pole,
and to those attacking a tin drain-pipe. My
persistence produced nothing but irritation.

Here was discouragement at the start, and
yet somehow it failed to close the question
satisfactorily. There was a final recourse.
I would write letters of inquiry to the most
eminent experts. My first reply added such
weight of discouragement that I deeply regretted the other letters already sent on their
absurd mission.

Zoological Park, New York.

"I never heard of such an occurrence as
was described to you in Maine. The information that was given you is certainly re-
markable—to say the least. I would not
venture to publish anything of the kind unless
I saw it myself; and even then I am not sure
that I would not doubt the evidence of my
own eyes!

"My disbelief is based on the ground that one or two, or even half a dozen holes such as a woodpecker could drill in a *green tree* could not possibly kill the tree. The sap-suckers do kill apple trees by drilling *an immense number* of holes in rings, completely around the trunk, and extending upward and downward for several feet. These holes, however, are exceedingly small—no larger than a slate-pencil—and as fast as a hole is dug and the sap extracted from it, another hole is bored in order to produce a fresh supply.

"I do not know of any tree in the North which produces any poisonous sap that would stupefy creatures as well organized and vigorous as woodpeckers. I advise you to regard the alleged observations as not proven!"

Sincerely yours,

"William T. Hornaday."

Although now convinced of the absurdity of my story in its main features, certain details seemed to be left in an unsatisfactory state. My poor little yarn should die hard, at any rate, so I gathered up its fragments and laid them out in the following reply to Mr. Hornaday:

"Thank you very much for your prompt

and definite letter. I should not bother you with further correspondence on this subject if it were not for the fact that you denied the only part of the woodpecker story which I know to be true. You say your disbelief is based on the ground that one, or two, or even half a dozen holes such as a woodpecker could drill in a green tree could not possibly kill the tree. There were two trees left in the clearing. I have been up there twice. The first time I went there one tree was dead, and as full of holes from top to bottom as a sieve. Let us assume that each was a dead tree in the first place, despite the statements of the campers there. The only tree that was perfectly good on my first visit I found on my second to be dying, and a great quantity of holes had appeared in the trunk and branches. In order to be thoroughly conservative, I will say that I have seen as many as twenty woodpeckers flying around there at one time. There is my data on which I would give oath. As to whether those disreputable birds killed the first tree, and had an orgy when they did it, and as to whether they alone are the cause of the dying condition of the second, I can offer only hearsay.

"The story disturbs my mind considerably.

I hate to tell it, because if I am to get the credit of being a liar I should like to fix up a real, thorough, complete, and artistic lie that is all my own; this one I cannot claim, and part of it is apparently the truth. What am I going to do about it?"

This letter brought the following reply:

"Your last letter is a puzzler, and I pass! I think you will be eminently justified in writing up the whole matter exactly as you saw it, and as it was reported to you by people whom you believe to be careful observers and also truthful. It seems quite apparent from the great number of holes that were drilled into those trees, that the birds really did kill the trees—a most unusual thing to happen in this part of the world, though common enough in California by a different procedure. It will be interesting to your readers to know the species of the trees that were killed, and any other details bearing upon the subject. . .

"Of course you will not fail to mention the species of woodpeckers that were connected with the episode you are going to describe, because that is quite important. Weigh carefully every observation reported to you by other persons, and if you can give the names of your informants it will be well to do so. This will throw the burden of proof of any statements of theirs that may be doubtful upon them, and not upon you.

"But by all means write your story and publish it. So far as I am aware, it will be absolutely new, and I can promise that at least one man in this part of the Bronx will read every word that you write."

Here was new incentive. Perhaps these inquiries might result in a contribution to science that would group my name with that of Audubon. But hard upon the heels of that friendly and stimulating letter came a confusion of replies that left me perplexed, my mind bruised by words that I could not pronounce, some of them at least sixteen letters long. Among them, however, were some wholly within my comprehension, and these I quote. For assuredly it is never wise or even safe to set down words one does not understand, though one should hedge them by a veritable bristle of quotation-marks.

"The story of woodpeckers getting drunk on fermented sap is an absurd fable. They drink the fresh sap.

"Yours truly,
"ERNEST THOMPSON SETON."

"Replying to yours of the 5th, I have never witnessed a scene such as you describe. The red-bellied woodpeckers do drill holes in live trees for the sap and for the soft inner bark, the cambium layer, but I have never known them to kill a tree. Both birds and insects might get drunk on the fermented sap.

"Very truly yours,

"JOHN BURROUGHS."

JOHNS HOPKINS UNIVERSITY.

"I am pretty familiar with the woodpecker, and I doubt if they are responsible for the foul work of which they are accused. So far as I know, a woodpecker never drives holes in a tree until a worm or insect has previously bored in. Whether the holes he drives are hard on the trees is another matter. I am inclined to think that it is better to have the worms and insects out, because the wound will heal. In my judgment trees would have died anyway.

"Now as to the lack of sobriety—I do not doubt that fermentation often takes place and that some of the birds, in search for food which had entered the old holes, might have taken too much of the fermented products.

I have seen robins in a 'loggy' condition upon very ripe berries in the South.

"With regrets that I cannot give you more exact information, I am

"Sincerely yours,
"JOHN B. WATSON."

DEPARTMENT OF AGRICULTURE,
WASHINGTON, D. C.

"In response to your request of July 11th, I take pleasure in forwarding a copy of Biological Survey Bulletin, No. 37.

"I think there can be no doubt as to the fact that occasionally woodpeckers destroy trees of considerable size, though naturally the principal damage they do is to young and rather small trees on which an equal amount of damage is, relative to the size of the tree, much greater.

"There is not the slightest doubt as to the sapsucker habitually drinking sap. Other species have been known to do the same thing, though not habitually.

"Very truly yours,
H. W. HENSHAW."

"I have just returned from the camp after a very pleasant stay of nearly five weeks.

I regret I am unable to add anything of import to the controversy regarding the behavior of the woodpeckers there. All of the large birch trees about the camp have been removed except one. The ones removed did not show that they had been untimely cut off by the acts of the birds, as they were very large and fully matured. The downy woodpeckers were at work on the remaining one, feeding on the inner bark. And my judgment is that they were not helping to prolong the life of the trees, as the scars they left were quite extensive. I only noticed two yellow-bellied sapsuckers about the camp; and, as there were no trees near to feed on, their behavior was quite proper. I am unable to pass an opinion as to what it might have been if they had an opportunity to get full.

"However, I hope there is someone who can settle this momentous question for all time. . . . .

"Yours truly,
"R. T. Greene."

Western Reserve University.
"I have never found or seen an intoxicated woodpecker, though I have heard the story that they occasionally get too heavy a load

of the fermented sap of their favorite trees. Before expressing or even entertaining an opinion on the probability of such an occurrence, I should wish to know the proportion of sugar in the sap of, say, the birch or the apple, if that tree also were in question. This I do not know, but doubt if sugar is present in sufficient quantity to produce the result described, and of course there could be no alcohol without sugar. There is another point: the woodpecker makes the holes on a vertical limb, and the sap flows out; this sap is of course fresh and unfermented, and could accordingly produce no such untoward result; the woodpecker goes away, but later returns and finds fermented sap, drinks, and falls down stupefied; that, I believe, is the idea. But, as you will see, this explanation is vulnerable at more than one point: a liquid cannot concentrate in a vertically placed hole, but will ooze out by capillary attraction as well as by gravity, and be quickly dissipated by evaporation; moreover the oozing will tend to keep the sap fresh in the hole made by the woodpecker, and where he is supposed to get his grog. So you see that such general considerations are not very favorable to the idea. Further, I am not at all sure that over-ripe fruits, when hanging to the bush or tree, undergo alcoholic fermentation; they certainly do not unless their skin is broken by force or decay; the general tendency is to shrink by drying, leading to a concentration of their juices, while they cling to the tree. . . .

> "Very sincerely yours,
> "FRANCIS H. HERRICK."

MERIDEN, N. H.

"I do not think it impossible, perhaps not improbable, that a woodpecker, at least a yellow-bellied woodpecker, might become stupefied by drinking the fermented sap of a birch tree. Birch sap constitutes a favorite and, at times, the principal food of this bird, and if for domestic or other reasons he were driven to drink it when it had fermented, it seems reasonable to believe that he might become intoxicated. Mr. Clifton W. Loveland, Ornithologist of the Rhode Island State Board of Agriculture, has observed that humming-birds and some squirrels which fed on sap flowing from pits made in birch trees by yellow-bellied woodpeckers appeared to be stimulated, while other squirrels were rendered loggy and stupid by drinking the same sap.

"Robins overtaken by late snow-storms in the spring, and reduced to eating the decayed apples which still hang on the trees, sometimes roll around on the snow, utterly helpless, apparently from the effects of the fermented apple-juice.

"A young black bear, with whom I had a close personal acquaintance, once showed all the usual signs of intoxication after having surreptitiously—or perhaps I should say syruptitiously—eaten all the molasses he could hold.

"I doubt if woodpeckers or other birds ever do *willful* mischief. That is to say, whatever damage or annoyance they may cause by their actions, I believe that those actions were performed without any intention of causing damage or annoyance, without even the knowledge that such damage and annoyance had been or could be caused by anything. Probably the primary object of the drumming of woodpeckers is to signal to other woodpeckers. The act is performed by hammering rapidly with the bill upon some resonant object. Formerly this object was usually a hard, dead branch or twig. But, like purple martins, chimney-swifts, and many other birds, the woodpeckers find that certain changes in their environment are advantageous to them, and take advantage of these changes. They have found that metal water-spouts, taut wire, tin cans, and perhaps screen-doors are more resonant than dead branches and drum upon them probably for that reason.

"In some cases it would appear that they have developed a taste for the music as well, and drum away, apparently quite indifferent as to whether they are heard by others of their kind or not. Sometimes, unfortunately, they select, and repeatedly visit, drumming-posts close to the abodes of people who do not appreciate that kind of music, and their innocent attempts to express themselves are mistaken for cussedness.

"Sincerely yours,
"ERNEST HAROLD BAYNES."

"Of course, we never had any expert opinion on the actions of the woodpeckers at ———Pond. The facts were these: a white birch tree standing in the clearing seemed to be especially attractive to a lot of woodpeckers—so much so that the attention of people in the camp was attracted to their antics.

The tree was giving forth lots of sap, and so far as we could judge the woodpeckers were attracted by it, as they gathered on the tree in numbers. They seemed to be stupefied— so much so that you could take a fishing-rod and poke at them and they would not leave the tree. People around the camp who watched them said they were intoxicated. The birds would fly to the tree as any bird would fly, apparently full of life and energy and after remaining there and apparently feeding upon this sap they became, as I have said, stupefied.

"The opinion that the sap had overpowered the birds was, of course, simply a layman's idea, but as a lawyer, familiar with the rules of evidence, I am certain I could convince a jury that the sap was responsible for their condition. Whether the circumstances would have any effect upon a body of scientists, I do not know. It certainly is a fact, however, that those people who visited the camp for two or three years while this was going on were firmly convinced that the woodpeckers ate the sap and that it dulled their faculties.

"Your faithfully,
"CHARLES N. CODDING."

Long before the arrival of the last word from these correspondents I had ceased to hope for a settlement of the original problem. What those Maine birds did or did not do would never be proved. But what a woodpecker or even a robin might do if tempted was a more interesting question. May there be in a bird's nature capabilities for mischief or crime I had not hitherto suspected? My eyes were opened to evidence. An item in the day's news caught my attention:

WOODPECKERS DESTROY CHURCH

ANCIENT EDIFICE IN PENNSYLVANIA VILLAGE PRACTICALLY WRECKED BY MISCHIEVOUS BIRDS

Can there be atheists among them? I have heard that there are kindly disposed people ready to devote funds for the establishment of cemeteries for pet birds and beasts. Do they not owe a greater duty to the living? Let them seek out woodpecker colonies where the moral tone is low, and provide funds for the maintenance among them of settlement-workers; gently bred canaries from clergymen's households might be drafted, if they would not volunteer.

These are but leaves from the notebook of an unscientific person; they arrive at no conclusions—not even a summing up; yet perhaps some passing scientist may find a grain of wheat among the chaff. As for myself, I seem to possess a changed attitude of mind toward the whole feathered tribe.

Professor Herrick's woodpecker acquaintance who drummed daily for more than a week on the roof of a neighbor's bird-house may have been calling his mates as that eminent scientist suggests, or he may have loved the music of his own making. But if I were asked to give an unscientific opinion upon the question, I should say, "Tell me first what family lived within that bird-house, and all that you may chance to know of the social gossip of that bird community."

Only a day or two ago we were waked at a very early hour by a woodpecker who rapped resoundingly on the wire netting of our front screen-door. No one can convince me that he sought food or drink; he was looking for trouble. To-day one flew to a tree close at hand, caught sight of me, and immediately put the tree trunk between us. One time I should have admired his plumage, felt some little pride because of his tameness, and given him no further thought. But now I dropped my rake and followed him around his tree-trunk, saying pleadingly: "You're up to something, old chap. Let me in on it, won't you? I'm a good fellow, myself."

IN A FAR-OFF LAND OF MEMORY

THE elusive scent of boxwood can transport me in spirit over some hundreds of miles of distance and thirty years of time; the heart-lifting thump of a bass drum is a magician's incantation, for it has power to turn me into a touseled boy with dragging shoestrings to prove his unpreparedness, trotting beside a circus band. But greater in magic power than either of these is a dry, cold, twilight morning before day has fully broken, silent and clear aired. The stillness of it, or the clear coolness, or the fresh verdury smell seize upon my heart and soul and whirl them away. Then upon my bodily eyes crowd these jostling houses with iron bound streets pushing between, and back fly heart and soul to the body that claims them. So swift has been the journey that I can scarcely be sure they went and came again. Yet now and then the magic of some twilight morning will have such power that my spirit goes forth deliberately, fully equipped, and wanders at will in a certain far-off land of memory, seeking out treasured scenes and situations and finding them real and true. As a dream fades with full waking, so fades the recollection of these Aladdin's journeys. Yet there are glimpses of that vague and distant land which I would snatch and hold.

Nearly always I may see it most clearly in the dusk before sunrise. The billowing plain is covered with a carpet of dull brown, figured with dots of duller green—and at the edge of the world in every direction are ragged purple mountains, strangely shaped and broken. Ah, the color of it all as the sun stirs, and the clearness—every cactus finger that points from earth on a neighboring billow crest is a sharp penciling upon the background of distant purple mountain sides. The vast silences are broken only by sounds that seem to accentuate silence—a rattling pebble, a crackling of dry stalks, a faint hoot that might be the far off shout of a man or the snort of a steer, and at wide intervals a long-drawn-out quavering cry answered by another, so faint as to seem but an echo inside the brain. Within this picture that I seize and hold there is one moving figure—a boy on horseback. He is in canvas "chapps" and grey sombrero, and guides his bony, mottled little steed uncertainly. First they surmount a billow of land ahead, only to turn perplexedly and gallop over some rise to the left or right. When the rein falls idle on her neck the spotted bronco halts; she is purposeless and carefree. But her rider is a half-frightened boy—lost in a world of infinite silences and limitless extent.

Just as the lad's anxiety is growing into actual fear, over the top of the crest immediately before him rises a high-crowned straw sombrero, and under it a dusky face with teeth that flash the signal of a glad smile— then the whole figure of rider and horse appears and the enveloping silence is broken by a shrill musical cry, "*A—qui! El grin—gito!*"

Side by side vacquero and boy trot their ponies, up and down the little hills in a direction that seems to the lad all wrong; now and then other riders with grinning friendly faces under their wide hat-brims pop up against the sky—and jocular unintelligible phrases are called out to the lad, whose carelessness on his first morning in the round-up camp has won them an hour's relief from the day's routine.

Certain well-defined figures dwell in that land of memory. The rest is a wonderful jumble of colors, sounds, and smells. Most clearly outstanding is big Alec Cloete—black-bearded South African with a Boer name, but English colonial from Stetson to boot spurs. I do not attempt to disguise him here, but only hope this may catch the eyes of others of his friends. He died in South Africa as heroically and tragically as a man may—saving a weaker life than his own. This is the humble tribute of a small boy who rode by his side and ate and slept with him through many revealing days behind the cattle. Big, boisterous, kindly, tender, impetuous, and utterly unfearing—he belonged in the open, for of such stuff has Britain built new colonies, and with such hands has she extended them.

Out of the circle of faces about him grins the ebony countenance of Jim the cook. Master of the buckboard commissariat, he built stew and biscuit of such raw material as he found at hand; sweetened thick coffee with raw black cane sugar when the neighborhood yielded it, or sweetened it not at all; buttered biscuit with bits of unpedigreed fat or again with a tin of pate-de-foi-gras—or buttered them not at all. Even of temper, yet marvelously profane with the worst of two languages at his command, he navigated his mules over a tempestuous sea, steering volubly down the side of some sudden wave with a force that hurled his rattling ship to the crest of the wave ahead, until a saddlesore boy who had sought ease beside him would flee, loosened in every joint, to the saddle again, while merry vacqueros hailed his return with jibes.

Memory gives a conglomerate picture of those companion riders, José and Pedro, Jesús, Santiago, Miguel—twenty or more— children in work or play, and work and play were all one to them. The breaking out from the herd of a frightened bunch of steers meant a yell and a race, large dramatics over small events—laughter and songs.

The singing comes back most vividly of all. In the evenings, with the cattle halted and the little herd of horses fed and then absurdly, yet sufficiently, fenced by a single strand of encircling rope, choruses would start here and there. There is no singing like it in settled places. The silence of an empty world round about demands repressed voices, and weird mysterious minor notes predominate. Now and then a high tenor leads the rest into a shrill crescendo; and so the music rises and falls, passionate or tender, while the firelight reveals this dusky face and that— here an Indian type, there a Spanish, some flat and emotionless, some handsome as Señor Don Adonis himself, and all throwing into the simple words they sang the wordless passion of this new mixed race.

Then, later on, the voices of the night— the memory of them now is elusive until some still, cool, brilliantly starlit hour of to-day sends them flooding back. There was the fitful lowing of cattle and the rattle of horns, —ceasing altogether for long periods, and then starting up again, as though a psychic disturbance spread out in ever widening circles from some central point to the edges of the herd. Often, in the intervening periods of stillness, one might hear the wailing, quavering bark of a coyote, echoed still more faintly by another, miles and miles away. Yet all these noises seemed but a form of silence, and made background for the plaintive singing of a single night guard riding slowly along the edges of the herd. Always these night watchers were singing. The mysterious black shape of a horse and rider coming suddenly out of the dark would have frightened a nervous wakeful steer, and started him and his companions crashing away in a dreaded night stampede. But the voices of men were commonplace by this time; and so the sentries sang to the cattle plaintive, high-keyed ballads, and a small boy lay awake and listened and listened.

There are times when imagination, and even reason, struggle against memory, and then a little collection of boyish letters comes to the rescue. It is hard now to form a mental picture of sixteen hundred steers. Stand them in a row, head to tail, single file, and they might reach from here to Timbuctoo, as popular statistics would put it, or they might not. Present-day experiences are of no avail in outlining the picture. But an old letter in a cramped schoolboy hand tells me that sixteen hundred head of cattle were cut out and counted from a vastly larger herd, and then driven northward for a hundred miles or more and swum across the river that divides that land from this.

There is some recollection of the counting of the cattle. Big Alec stood idly, it seemed, now and then speaking a word of direction, while a group of mounted vacqueros made a

gateway of their own number and spread the
herd out in a long stream that swept past
the chief at a trot, now in tens, now in thirties
and forties, ploughing into each other, snorting, jumping, retarded occasionally while
two belligerent fellows locked horns, and
then dashing on past at greater speed. All
this time their owner was counting, yet the
only indications of his close attention were
his busy hands. In one he held a number of
pebbles, and as he reached a certain unit a
pebble would shift from one hand to the
other; and I remember that he did not err
as to the total by so much as a single head.

Perhaps one reason that the early mornings
live most vividly in mind is that so much of
interest happened then, just at the dawn.
There was the breakfast, and the breaking
of camp, the choosing and roping of the day's
mount, and the always thrilling moment
when the herd was set in motion again.
Strange creatures, those steers, with more
of ratiocination than it had seemed to me a
cow might possess. They had lived on a
piece of territory as large as one of our small-
est American states, and had roamed unmo-
lested for more than a year. Their section
of open country was absolutely undistinguish-

able in character and appearance from adjacent sections, yet the moment they crossed the line where their northern fence had been they were nervous, ready to listen to false rumors, disturbed by the signal of a snake's rattle, or even by the breaking of a stick, stampeding anywhere if not controlled. Yet, now and then, when little groups got wholly away, and men who could not be spared were called back from the pursuit, the lost cattle would finally swing about, and take up the trail of their fellows; perhaps twenty-four hours later they would come drifting in, weary and repentant.

But the personality of those steers comes back to mind not half so clearly as the human-like qualities of the bony little horses whose duty it was to guard them. The picture is vivid of a small boy, promoted to an actual place in the riding line, suddenly awake to the fact that half a dozen head of cattle had broken from the herd for some mysterious cause, and were dashing sharply to the left, into the brush. With a joyous yell, imitating the example set by his professional comrades, the lad turned sharply after them, but found to his amazement that his spotted steed refused to accept guidance. Instead of following the truants she turned almost at right angles to their trail, and utterly regardless of the rein on her neck or even of the bit in her teeth, darted on this tangent, apparently without goal or purpose. After perhaps five minutes, still without consideration of her youthful rider's wishes, she brought around in a half circle, right into the path of the wanderers, headed them off, turned them, and trotted placidly behind them until they rejoined the herd. It was hard not to believe that in her mind there was contempt for the inexperienced youth upon her back. It was pleasanter to feel that she had gained a definite affection for him, and was determined, so far as lay within her power, to see that he did not reap the humiliation that was the proper reward for his errors. Certain it was that she, more than any human comrade, trained him into such small usefulness as he attained.

One legend of the plains firmly fixed in a small boy's mind died at that time a sudden death. The bucking bronco and the mount whose temper made him unreliable were not in evidence. The rider who leapt upon a dancing steed and overpowered him in spite of rearings and chargings had no place in the busy routine of a round-up and drive. The horse that might risk the life of a man or the loss of cattle was shot. This does not mean that the survivors were gentle, plodding beasts, of a placid disposition. They were live, swift, and alert, knowing the day's work as well as their masters, and sometimes, it seemed, almost capable of doing it alone.

Prejudice, too, rebels at some of the least important recollections of a day's drive. It is hard to believe now that one could ever greet with a yell of delight the sight of a water hole that had been crossed by a thousand cattle, where the liquid that had once been clear water was churned into a soup of mire, and that man and boy would kneel without a thought of objection, and drink this material until thirst was quenched.

Imagination rebels at memory's description of the biscuit, and even memory records that for a day or two a small boy's stomach was half empty, and that he felt a hunger he did not dare admit.

Prejudice also rebels at the memory of the rattlesnakes. The occasional scorpion and tarantula somehow seem more reasonable. But it is hard now to believe that even a happy-go-lucky lad could spend a night on a bit of ground that had been searched for snakes before camp was made, and that had perhaps yielded up two or three fat serpents; yet the lad himself brought home an enormous skin that he had stripped from such a trophy and stuffed with cornmeal purloined from Jim's buckboard. Mice ate the cornmeal, and showed scant respect for the skin that held it, but it had lasted long enough to be a steady trial to the mistress of a civilized and tidy home.

There was a belief among the vacqueros that a rattler in his death fight would turn and bite his own flesh, and if this happened the whole snake's body was poisoned. In the killing they guarded against this with the greatest care, and in the cowboy camp there was no greater delicacy than the tender snake meat of the unbitten snake, roasted over the camp fire. Memory boldly asserts that the flavor was a pleasant mean between the white meat of a chicken and some firm-fleshed type of fish.

Amid the kaleidoscopic colors of many brilliant days and nights I picture that small boy moving in a company of workers more like children than himself. For the faint rumble as of thunder and the tremble of the earth beneath his head that more than once roused him in the night brought fear with it as well as excitement. In him was a nascent Anglo-Saxon sense of responsibility. Each stampede meant possible loss of cattle and valuable hours wasted. But his companions played a joyous game, with excitement as its only stake; even the pay at the end of the journey meant simply more excitement. They were as irresponsible as children, and to him they seemed as lovable. Readily, at any challenge, they swung into a race, swinging sombreros, yelling merrily; often some angry steer that had strayed and refused to be driven back became "el toro," with a circle of hilarious amateur *picadors* and *toreadors* leaping about him, until such time as Big Alec thought it best to discover their truancy.

Pedro may now be "el capitan" somewhere in that sorrowful land, with silver beads on his sombrero, riding as fearlessly and as merrily and as irresponsibly in some factional raid, at the beck of a mongrel leader. Miguel may be opposing his old comrade, if luck so has it, with silver filagree on his skintight trousers and a Mauser at his shoulder, caring not a picayune for his own life or any other. And the survivor of them will

shout *"Viva liberdad,"* or *"Viva constitucion,"*
and that evening, thrumming his guitar in
a doorway, will sing tender plaintive melodies
to the brilliant stars.

What an emotional, affectionate, cruel, childlike, crazy people; ever ready to be led, with
the worst products of their breed for leaders!
Ever too ready for play; and self-seekers
even on this side of the river, God forgive us,
have been too ready to supply them with
bloody games to play at.

What a histrionic, praiseloving people!
Putting more than the cost of a house and
furniture into adornment for a hat, they
strut, they fight, they gamble, they serenade
their loves with an orchestra of assistants.
I cherish the memory of a later time in that
romantic land when a gaudily dressed Cyrano
went beneath his lady's window with a string-
band to prove his devotion. And because
Providence had deprived him of a singing
voice, a *camerado* beside him sang passionate
words while he at fitting moments made mute
appealing gestures in the moonlight. But that
is a picture of the towns, where a somewhat
different people dwell; it has no rightful place
among these eluding memories of a small boy
riding through the hills beside the cattle.

With all his pride of employment it was little else than play to the lad who was a child in years rather than in race. He galloped after dodging jack-rabbits, or took futile pot shots at some wise old thief of a coyote which trailed the buckboard, just out of rifle range. He waked one night with a yell of alarm because a wild beast roared in his very ear, and found a little donkey standing over him, hee-hawing expressions of curiosity while his long ears wagged against the moon. That was a joke on *el gringito* to feed the very souls of Pedro, Santiago, Jesús, and Miguel for days to come.

As they rode forward the background of the picture changed somewhat from hour to hour. The dull brown dry earth, spotted with the green of many-shaped cacti, would give place to brighter green groves of low prickly mesquite trees, and those groves would in their turn give place to bits of cultivated land here and there, with simple systems of irrigation marking the slopes like a checker-board. In such a neighborhood the chief would negotiate with some pompous hidalgo in his mud house for replenishment of the buckboard, and his payment would include such sugar-cane as the merry vacqueros might steal in passing. This was much as an indulgent father might do if he paid a farmer in advance, *en bloc*, for the apples and cucumbers his children were sure to purloin through the coming summer. The sugar-cane was sweeter to these grown-up children if they did not know that it had been purchased in advance.

Simple hearted, I called them, and it comes to mind that years later, in a more southern part of that land of memory, we rode down a mountain side and met a snake-like caravan of little donkeys, each loaded with crates of brilliant yellow oranges. They were bound for the market place of the distant city, so their various drivers told us as we passed them. We stopped them, one after another, and negotiated for a crate. "But no," each owner would say, obstinately, "These are for sale in the market."

"What will you get for them there?"

"Ah, who knows? Perhaps one peso for such a crate as this."

"Here is your peso. Give us the oranges."

"*Nada*" (nothing doing), with a negative shake of the fore-finger, "Why should I drive an idle burro from here to the market-place? You may buy more down the mountain where these came from."

"Then a *peso* and two *reals* for your trouble."

"*Nada, nada*, what should I be doing with an empty-backed burro, coming into the market-place?"

Such were the children of that land of memory. And so Santiago, Pedro, Miguel, and the rest raced and gamboled, shouted and sang in their ride northward; and steadily northward rode Big Alec, and Jim with his buckboard, and the sixteen hundred head of cattle, with scarcely a single pair missing from that tossing, flashing forest of curling horns; until one day at dawn they looked down on the winding path of the river that marked the boundary line between two nations. Of all the vivid early morning pictures, there was painted on that day the most vivid of all. A few steers that had proved themselves foremost in stampeding or mischievous truancy were forced into the lead. The whole army of cattle was then driven down the gentle slope; crowding, pushing, climbing forward onto the very backs of slower beasts ahead, they rushed with increasing momentum toward the river bank.

At the brink they hesitated, but behind them came the others, crowding forward. At the effective moment, splash had gone Big Alec and his horse into the stream. After went the leaders of the herd, following the horse that led them. It must have been no easy matter for horse and rider to stay in mid-river, keep out of the path of those frightened cattle, and at the same time turn stragglers, heading weakly down stream with the current, so that all would keep in an orderly line to the easy bit of low shore on the other side. With their usual joyous dramatics, José and Miguel and all the rest leapt into the current from the bank here and there with the last of the herd. It was a wonderful sight as the trailers plunged in—a river filled with tossing ivory horns, under them blood-shot eyes, and mouths snorting and blowing in excitement; and on the other shore an emerging herd, neatly turned against itself and "milled" to prevent a stampede. When the small boy stood on that far bank and found the same brown carpet of earth, spotted here and there with the dull green of many-shaped cacti, even in his immature mind large thoughts formed themselves as he looked back at that other land. It looked so like,